Edna O'Brien

Mother Ireland

with photographs by Fergus Bourke

Weidenfeld and Nicolson   London

First published by Weidenfeld and Nicolson
11 St John's Hill London SW11

Designed by Tim Higgins

Filmset by Keyspools Ltd Golborne Lancashire
Printed in Great Britain by
Cox & Wyman Ltd
London, Fakenham and Reading

ISBN 0 297 77110 8

For John Fortune – then

Contents

Acknowledgments

I am bound to thank many friends in Ireland for the help they have given me in writing this book, but I doubt that I could have managed it at all without the kindness and assistance from Fiac O'Broin. Two teachers, Patrick Vaughan and John Jones, loaned me their precious school books. I should also like to thank John Montague for allowing me to quote two poems from his *Faber Book of Irish Verse*. The Country itself did the rest. But I must stress that only half the book is my doing, the other half belonging to the photographer Fergus Bourke.

Illustrations

'Let me say before I go any further
that I forgive nobody. I wish them all
an atrocious life and then the fires
and ice of hell and in the execrable
generations to come an honoured name.'

Malone Dies by Samuel Beckett

1 The land itself

COUNTRIES are either mothers or fathers, and engender the emotional bristle secretly reserved for either sire. Ireland has always been a woman, a womb, a cave, a cow, a Rosaleen, a sow, a bride, a harlot, and, of course, the gaunt Hag of Beare. Originally a land of woods and thickets, such as Orpheus had seen when prescribing the voyage of Jason, through a misted atmosphere. She is thought to have known invasion from the time when the Ice Age ended and the improving climate allowed deer to throng her dense forest.

These infiltrations have been told and fabricated by men and by mediums who described the violation of her body and soul. Ireland has always been Godridden. St Patrick, her patron saint (uncanonised!) fled as a slave from Antrim in answer to a voice that told him to join a ship and go to the Continent. He travelled with a consignment of Irish wolfhounds and got off in France, where at Auxerre, he studied to be a cleric. Again a voice accompanied by a vision summoned him back to Ireland and in the fifth century he began to convert the North, then the lowlands, so that the speech and thinking of men changed as they fell under Patrick's rule and the yoke of the Scriptures. Patrick's forbears, the Romans, did not invade Ireland, but Tacitus records how a Roman general gazed across the sea from Scotland and reckoned that a single legion could have subdued her. He was possibly mistaken, for despite the many other legions that tried to subdue her, Ireland was never fully taken, though most thoroughly dispossessed.

Around 1860, a nun of a contemplative order in County Kerry spent her time compiling her country's history as an incitement to Irishmen and Irishwomen in America to remind them of their noble and glorious annals. She stressed how Ireland had never apostatised. As a recluse she found it necessary to defend herself from the smear of patriotism. She felt that a patriot heart might burn just as ardently beneath the veil as beneath the coif! She cited the example of Michael O'Cleirgh, a friar, who in the 1600s worked on *The Annals of the Four Masters* to set down the history of his sorrowful race, 'so that it would survive unto the end of the world'.

Taking her brief from him she described the first taking of the Void Erinn in the days before the flood, when a Hebrew woman, a lady, Caesara, niece of Noah, hearing her uncle's prophecy about a universal flood, decided to seek refuge in some foreign region, hoping to find a country as yet uninhabited and so with sin unspotted. She set out with a flock of three men and fifty women, sailing through the Red Sea, by the altars of the Philistines with the pillars of Hercules as beacons; past the treacherous coast of Spain, to Ireland, Isle of Destiny, on the shift for sustenance. Her people are the first to be interred there, the first in a long line of hardy Irish ghosts.

There followed the taking by the Partholans, Scions of the sons of Japhet, who reached her by way of the Mediterranean and the Atlantic three hundred years after the deluge, in about the year 2000 of the world. They arrived in Kenmare in the west of Munster and are thought to have disseminated letters, commerce and agriculture. To their king, Partholan, is accorded the first instance of jealousy in Ireland. His wife had been guilty of a pleasant intrigue with one of her slaves and when rebuked for this, she asked her husband did he think that one may leave honey near a woman, sweet milk near a child, food near a man, flesh meat near a cat, tools near a mechanic, man near a woman in a desert, and that they would ignore one another? In fury he seized her favourite hound and dashing it against the ground he killed it

His people died from the plague, leaving the land extinct. Then came Nemedh, of the posterity of Magog, and hardly had that tribe installed themselves on the island than the Formorains came, monstrous mariners from Africa, who demanded of their subjects taxes, in the form of children, corn, cattle, cream, butter and flour.

They were invaded and ousted by the Firbolgs, the men of the paunchy stomachs who came from Greece in consequence of a bondage inflicted by their masters, which was that they had to carry bags of clay on them, in order to spread earth onto rocks. They divided Ireland into five parts, each part constituting a kingdom, and they lived in peace until the Druids came around the year 3000 on a fair May morning. The Druids, versed in magic and wizardry, were called the Tuatha de Danann, being under the reign of the magic goddess Dana. They possessed four talismans of high power, a stone of destiny that roared upon the election of a king, a long sword that knew no defeat, a spear of equal propensity, and a boiling cauldron for punishments. Yet for them too, the evening of their magic came and they were overwhelmed and driven underground by the sons of Milesius, the Gaels who came from Spain.

The Dananns had first defeated them by throwing a mist over the island so that it seemed to assume the shape of a hog's back and by sending their three queens to cajole and confuse the Milesians. A bargain was struck. The Milesians would journey nine 'tonnes' out to sea and if a second time they succeeded in making a landing then they had sovereignty of the land.

But once at sea the Dananns raised a destructive tempest and stirred up a dreadful commotion of the waters so that vessels were struck and juggled like balls, the bulk of the crew drowned including the five sons of Milesius. Those who survived knew that the Dananns had tampered with the elements and returned with fresh reinforcements from Spain. They fought a pitched battle at Derry where they slaughtered the Danann warriors and also the Danann queens.

The Milesians partitioned the land between two brothers, Eber and Erimhon, each reigning for one year until they disputed the ownership of three vantage hills and in the inevitable battle Eber was slain. Erimhon then became King of Ireland, succeeded by a long line of kings until Macha, a woman of red tresses, claimed her right as lawful descendant. She disguised herself as a leper, charmed her possible male opponents into the woods, one by one, where she bound them in fetters and had them made slaves.

The hill of Tara in County Meath was the seat of inauguration of those kings and also the place where laws were promulgated or recited, annals added to, and genealogies brought up to date. Tara of the green mounds, palisaded and dyked, Tara with its stone of destiny and inherent hallowedness, was where the kings learned their many taboos and the prescriptions that would bring them good luck – the fish of the Boyne, the deer of Luibneck, the bilberries of Brileith, the cress of Brossnach, water from a well and the hares of Naas.

The conventions were always occasions of roistering and the high king, the sub-kings, their bodyguards, the poets, the lawyers, the women and the slaves all sat in their appointed places wearing the colours appropriated to them. A slave was permitted to wear one colour, a peasant two, a soldier three, a public victualler five, a king and poet six. Their chess pieces could pierce a man's brain and often did. Warriors sat down with their opponents' slain heads under their belts and guts falling about their feet while the common soldiers stuffed moss into their wounds to discourage the blood flow. 'Gold was not received as retribution from a man but his soul in one hour.' Yet they had their protocol, the niceties alongside the gore. When the cooked beast was cut up, the historian would be given a crooked bone, the hunter a pig's shoulder, the bard and the king the choicest fillets, and the smith the head of the beast! Eventually it was cursed by St Ruadhan in the year of our Lord 565, because the High King Diarmuid had ignored a right of sanctuary that was afforded to criminals in sacred places. The saint travelled from Tipperary, with his companies, stood on the Rath of Synods in Tara and put a curse on the king and the place with the result that it ceased to be a royal residence.

Tara now is a deserted unassuming place, with argument between the Board of Works and a lady who refuses to sell her share saying it does not constitute a national monument. You pass a tea house, a garden filled with postcard flowers, you pay a nominal entrance fee, climb the hill, you see that the stained glass window in the church has been smashed in, you go on climbing, you come to a stone edifice, you try to read the plaque documented in Irish, you look down and there are the bullocks on the plains below, and underneath you see the marks of where they have been digging for phenomenal finds. Six miles away is a holiday camp where girls in plastic hair rollers parade up and down the small toy-like concrete paths, looking for a Mister Right and ironically enough finding only distraught fathers hauling their children in and out of a Mickey Mouse show. Thomas Moore's poem though fanciful, is in spirit true and not wholly invalid either for the rest of Ireland:

> *The harp, that once thro' Tara's Halls,*
> *The soul of music shed,*
> *Now hangs as mute on Tara's walls*
> *As if that soul were fled.*
> *So sleeps the pride of former days,*
> *So glory's thrill is o'er....*

It was inevitable that Ireland should be invaded by the powerful Saxons, her neighbours across the Irish Sea, but the actual reason for that first foray is put down to human frailty. They made their first conquest in

1169, under the reign of Henry II and that because of an irony. Devorgilla, wife of Breifne O'Rourke, being enamoured of Dermot MacMurrough, Prince of Leinster, took advantage of her husband's absence and yielded herself to Dermot to have love and lust satisfied. When the cuckolded O'Rourke heard of this wrong, he went to the High King Rothorike and got aid to invade Leinster. Dermot's own assembly refused to help him and so he deserted his palace and fled to enlist help from Henry II, King of England, and was received with grace and benevolence into the king's bosom. The king gave him a document to take to Bristol in order to summon an army that would help him retrieve Leinster, and after much perseverance and much connivance Dermot got an army under a Robert Fitzstephens. With the promise of Wexford and two cantreds of land, Fitzstephens gathered together three score armed men, about three hundred archers, footmen well chosen and well piked. Embarking for Ireland they fulfilled the old prophecy of Merlin that she would be conquered by a knight biparted, since Fitzstephens had a Norman father and a Camber mother, and since his arms and insignia were divided by two mottoes. They filled the ditches around Wexford with the armed men, while the archers marked the turrets of the walls and from inside they were repulsed by the natives with great pieces of timber and stone. That night they withdrew and some of their ships were burnt, but on the morrow, having heard divine service, they gave a new assault and the citizens through the mediation of bishops and honest men gave in, offered hostages and promised loyalty to MacMurrough.

The footmen brought him three hundred enemy heads, which they laid at his feet, and turning every one of them to know them, he did then for joy hold up his hands, thank God and, seeing one head that was of a man he mortally hated, he held it by the hair and the ears and with his teeth bit away the nose and the lips. They continued their sallies through Leinster, fighting the brute Irish who came out of the woods, straits, passes and bogs, only to be slain in great numbers or have their heads cut off by the gallowglasses' axes. They murthered, spoilt, burnt and laid low so that

Mother Ireland   *Ah! light lovely lady with delicate lips aglow,*
With breast more white than a branch heavy-laden with snow,
When my hand was uplifted at Mass to salute the Host
I looked at you once, and the half of my soul was lost.

Cut turf   The turf built into ricks to dry. When burned the turf's smoke fills the room

...vith a beautiful aroma but also it itches people's eyes.

A hill of Donegal

Donegal – the brooding black
mountain, the untilled and
untillable fields, little farmhouses
tumbling down from the dizzying
slopes. For trees the conifer, for
colour the heather, and the
various plastic bags to bring
home cut turf. The sea, a charnel
black and the many lakes a blue
not unlike that of new galvanise.
An awesome place.

The West   Rich in folklore and tradition but poor in soil. Thomas Carlyle saw
in it nothing but beggary and stone. He differed not from Cromwell who
sent the natives there as an alternative to hell. Today's population
consists of 391,000 souls, of whom 75,000 are bachelors.

Dry stone wall, Connemara

The depopulated West – stony and barren as a quarry. The sheep nibble whatever there is and occasionally behind a wall one sees a small patch of green oats, like a little gaming table in the midst of crag.

Potato plants

The potato, regarded as the staple Irish diet – featured in everyone's description of the place, how the big pot was flung out on the kitchen table, the potatoes eaten in their skins, from the hand, without knife, fork or plate and with buttermilk as an accompaniment. If there was no buttermilk, they substituted by putting an onion in a jug of water both for flavour and milkiness. The two drastic years of 1847 and 1848 when blight

hit the potato crop the population was reduced by half, and Ireland at this time was described by the author William Carlton as being 'one vast lazar house filled with famine, disease and death'. Today, potato dishes include Colcannon, poundies, jacket potatoes, pan-fried potatoes, scalloped potatoes, parsley potatoes, Uisce Beathe (whiskey) potatoes, straw potatoes, potato nests, boxtie and fadge.

Tinker woman and her son

The Tinker Tribes are the Claffeys, the Sherlocks, the Driscolls, the Caseys, the Carthys, the Coffeys and the McQueens. They meet once a year at Killorglin in County Kerry, for the Puck Fair. There is Gathering Day, Fair Day and Scattering Day, during which a he-goat receives a tinsel crown in commemoration of some pagan rite.

those who thought to resist MacMurrough were obliged to re-think because, as the world knows, 'as fortune so the faith of man doth stand or fall'. The following year in 1170, Dermot then sent for Strongbow, Richard de Clare, luring him hither in language sweet as a girl's.

> Storks and swallows, as also the summer birds are come, and with the westerly winds have gone again [he wrote]. We have long looked and wished for your coming, and albeit the winds have been at east and easterly, yet hitherto you are not come unto us, wherefore now linger no longer, but hasten yourself hither with speed that it may therefore appear not want of goodwill, nor forgetfulness of promise, but the injury of time had been hitherto the cause of your long stay. All Leinster is already wholly yielded unto us, and if you will speedily come away with some strong company in force, we doubt not but that the other four portions will be received and adjoined to this first portion.

In secret he agreed with Rothorike, that as soon as Leinster was quelled he would return and send him all English people, and also not procure any more to come over. That plan never came to fruition. Soon after, Dermot died of an insufferable and unknown disease and his obituary says he had become putrid while living and died without penance, without the body of Christ, and without unction, as his evil deeds deserved.

The English stayed and according to the historian Sylvester Giraldus Cambrensus, a Gerald of Wales, they did so at great risk to their persons, not only in battle but in coming into contact with the savage Irish they were in danger of degeneration, as though they had tasted of Circe's poisoned cup.

Cambrensus was Godfearing by his own avowal in everything but his attitude to Ireland and the fair sex. He singled out their variable and fickle natures, using as chief target that villainess Cleopatra who got Antony 'to discard his wonted manners and to consume his time in vitious disorder and loose living'. Ireland he examined in body, soil and soul, according to his gnarled principles, and proclaimed the people, the 'rude' Irish, to be blind, loose, untameable, superstitious, religious, execrable, whiskey-swilling, frivolous, frank, amorous, ireful and gloating in war. Taking his leave of her he cursed her heartfully believing he was executing God's will. He wished her lands to burn, her breasts to be hungry, her wolves to famish upon the roadside. That curse was eventually brought to bear. A heavy and just judgment he delivered upon those parochial stiff-necked people who had refused to serve God in true religion, who resisted the anointing of the Lord and worshipped instead that wicked anti-Christ, the Pope of Rome.

The English, having settled themselves in the land did by degrees greatly diminish the woods in all places to deprive the native thieves and rogues of their refuge and starting holes. There followed colonisation, decimation, rebellion, counter-rebellion, laws, impaling, statutes, the atrocities of Cromwell, and the driving of the Irish across to Connaught where the land was rock with only sprigs of grass, herbs and harts tongue protruding between the fissures for the animals to feed on.

Dean Swift, who could tell one madman from another just as he could tell one gombeen from another, said that Ireland's misfortunes were not altogether her own fault but owing to a million of discouragements.

He set down the particulars of her rape, pointing out that as a nation she did not receive the timbers of the woods, neither for dwelling house nor trading ship, that one half of her whole income was clean profit to England, that families paying huge rents lived in filth and upon buttermilk and potatoes, that the king never came, and the viceroy stayed away for four-fifths of the year and that in short she could be likened 'to a patient who had physic sent by doctors at a distance'.

Everyone had something to say about her – essayists and travellers and attorneys and papal nuncios and lord chief justices – all said what they thought or what they assumed, and so we are to believe that the Irish were cordial, were headstrong, were penurious, that the 'vulgar' were inclined to drink beer and use quebath (whiskey) in excess, that men, women and children were addicted to a tobacco which they smoked in pipes two inches long and passed around with the word '*Shagh*', that they were prone to coughs, stopping of breath, looseness of thighs, rickets and the flux, that they put laurel leaves in the beer to flavour it, and ground their barley between two stones, that no reptiles were found there, or if imported nevertheless perished at once. The cabins or muck-heaps they lived in had walls the height of a man, with supporting rafters patched with straw and leaves, no chimneys and no windows so that the inmates near choked with the smoke. The vulgar Irishwomen's garments were loose-bodied and without any manner of stiffening, and they never wore bodices to check or direct the course of nature! They defended their heads from the heat of the sun and the onslaught of the rains with a mantle. Their eating was brutishness itself – they held of certainty that barnacles were flesh, they put the butter into wicker baskets and buried it in a bog to make provision for the fastings of Lent and then ate it stinking. At fairs a man ate a chop out of his hand without salt or sauce, and they even took salmon without vinegar. Ireland was always looked upon as a freak with nevertheless a fascination bordering on gluttony for the outsider.

A Doctor Twiss who landed there in 1775 said that 'as to their natural history they are remarkable for the thickness of their legs, especially those of plebeian females'. He then went on to say that those ladies, far from being disgustedly reserved, were very engaging and that a traveller having but little time to remain with them endeavoured to spend it as agreeably as he could. At Muckross Abbey in Killarney he got the jitters having just been beguiled by craggy rocks, shady valleys, verdant lawns and a yew tree shedding a dim religious light. He heard the Irish howl which was the bellowing of mourners at a wedding and he ran for his life. The papal nuncio's secretary praised the oysters having just bought a thousand for twelve and a half pence, and also bought a nag for five pounds which in Italy he reckoned would have cost him a hundred gold pieces.

A hundred years later, William Makepeace Thackeray was more sensibly disposed, finding them humble and loving of great folks. He described Dublinites cronying to small dignitaries up in the Phoenix Park which is called the Phaynix. Thackeray didn't excel in giving tips and this brought him plenty of odium from boots, waiters and postboys across the land. He saw and described Dublin's dirty faces, behind Dublin's dirty windows, children on all the broken steps, old men, 'smutty slipshod women', and beggars with Hogarthian faces. He went down to the Linen Hall and had sense enough to see that it was huge, useless, lonely, and decayed, and that the statue of George IV pointing to some bales of shirting was atrophy indeed. Some others like Mrs Arsenath Nicholson, an American lady who in 1844 went to investigate the conditions of the Poor, saw a people purified and unhurt, lavish kindness, and exultant dusk-haired beauties gathering for crossroad dancing to the sound of the bagpipes.

People fall in love with Ireland. They go there and are smitten, see the white cottages nestling so to speak beneath the hills, the ranges of brooding blue mountain, the haze above them, the fuchsia hedges in Kerry, the barking dogs, the chalky limestone steppes of west Clare, a phenomenon so unyielding it is as if Wuthering Heights were transmitted from paper to landscape. The visitors talk and are talked at, they fish, they fowl, they eat brown bread, dip into holy wells, kiss wishing stones, are bowled over but have no desire to stay. There must be something secretly catastrophic about a country from which so many people go, escape, and that something alongside the economic exigencies that sent over a million people in coffin ships when a blight hit the potato crops in 1847 and has been sending them in considerable numbers ever since.

Loneliness, the longing for adventure, the Roman Catholic Church, or the family tie that is more umbilical than among any other race on earth? The martyred Irish mother and the raving rollicking Irish father is not peculiar to the works of exorcised writers but common to families throughout the land. The children inherit a trinity of guilts (a Shamrock): the guilt for Christ's Passion and Crucifixion, the guilt for the plundered land, and the furtive guilt for the mother frequently defiled by the insatiable father. All that scenery, all those undercurrents are too much. There is a hopelessness that a glut of natural beauty can create when there is a cultural and intellectual morass. The question is not where have all the fairies gone but where are all the thinkers now.

Irish people do not like to be contradicted. Foiled again and again they have in them a rage that comes at you unawares like a briar jutting out of a hedge. There are those who cannot forget the past and there are those only too eager to forget it and bury it in one of the much sanctified deep freezes. Maude Gonne McBride, patriot and one whose beauty was a continuous inspiration to W. B. Yeats, saw the heart of Ireland as being powerfully alive and invisibly peopled but then she saw things that less psychic mortals could not apprehend. The country is breathlessly beautiful but there is too an undeniable sadness, the sadness of being cut off, the sadness of rabid materialism, jerry building, visual barbarities and a cultural atrophy that goes all the way to the brain. The new poems and new plays are few indeed and represent either small voices that are sad with their own alienation, or works of such tastelessness that they are indexes of the mass psyche of a people who are throttled. No great philosophers, no great psychiatrists, no achievement where logic is paramount; a great literary endowment, true, but lean offerings over the past thirty or forty years.

Romantic Ireland, quite dead, you say, when you are sitting down to high tea in Athlone, imploded with drop scones, apple pie and soda bread. It is here you recall that the Brown Bull of Ulster gored the White Bull of Connaught, left his loins by the water and hence Ath Luaine, the ford of the loins. When he drank elsewhere he left his opponent's liver, and elsewhere the shoulder-blades, and so on scattering the joints and the entrails, giving each place the name of whatever offering. After he had torn up the ground and died, Medb, Warring Queen of Connaught, made peace with Ulster and for seven years none of the Irish people were killed.

Athlone had the usual traffic jam, a poster announcing the drama festival and beside it one for a sheepdog trial. The cathedral was there, the rampart walls, and as in every Irish town toasted sandwiches from the infra grill. You read how there would be a festival and that the main attraction would be a beauty competition, ballads and extended licensing laws. You were in the centre of Ireland not far from the monastery of Clonmacnoise which at school you had read of as being a quiet watered land, a land of roses fair. You drove to the next town – similar streets, pile-up, a four-faced clock telling conflicting times, a drunk man with a mouth organ doing a jig, a lorry delivering calor gas refills and one of the Gardai studying the licence number of a parked car since in this era of terrorism nowhere is safe now from the brown paper parcel or the rag doll bomb.

'They drive like they fuck, any old way,' so the driver himself tells you, ignoring his own inconsistency and the speed that alters with the motion of his thoughts. He tells you another thing and it's this, that priests are mingling with the common people and that a priest had his 'hall door' out at a wedding in Limerick and did everything bar ask the bride to go to bed with him. For this he wants to register your facial expression and gives you the benefit of himself full face. You point to the wheel and quite openly stare down at a newspaper.

Most Reverend Dr Lucey, Bishop of Cork, fears that the country is not in danger of pollution from the oil rigs of Bantry Bay but that there is much more to dirty the minds of the people and to pollute their souls in the books, papers and films circulating through Ireland. Elsewhere you read that in fact due to a faulty valve two thousand five hundred gallons of oil spilled into the sea and a local councillor tossed the matter aside saying it did no great damage and that the Lord was on their side and that somebody must have been saying their prayers.

The driver prattles on. How he makes a point of bedecking his hire car with ribbons for weddings, that he is also in the secondhand clothing business and therefore able to divulge that big clothes are the most sought after because the country women are bulky from their intakes of starch. 'Fine imposing building,' he says as you pass what is either a barracks, a school, or a reformatory. It's 'by jingo' to everything and non-stop conversation and you ask yourself what is the deaf wish of the people of Ireland.

Rain again, wet fields, wet walls, rainbows arcing across the heavens, the perennial pebble or brick bungalow that the minister for local government extols as contributing to the variety of the Irish landscape. The clouds and the crows above are at odds with one another. Every so often a huge white plaster statue, with neon halo, a Jesus or a Mary or that flawless creature the Maid of Erin with hands outstretched.

Past the red and yellow consignment of tar barrels that are to signify work in progress and wan waves from solitary children going home dragging their satchels. Farmhouse accommodation everywhere and signs about fishing rights. Past a new chapel of variegated cement with colours as synthetic as jelly. Whirligigs and awful ceramic tiles above a new café and then hideous surprises such as a herd of cattle or a tractor tumbling out onto a main road and the driver declaring that that was the Divil altogether.

The journey is supposed to be northward to the seat of Connor, King of Ulster, but is suddenly interrupted when one of the other passengers in the back yells, 'Smoke, smoke'. Your man rushes out without turning off the ignition, rushes back to say he saw the smoke too but didn't like to remark on it in case he thought he might be seeing something. A garage, a mile away, yields nothing but a youth bearing an egg saucepan of water just poured onto the engine with a flourish, with the driver predicting she'd be all right, that she'd lick it. Without any prior consultation the men then repair to the nearside of a shed to relieve themselves and you are left to think of Connor who had lodged in his skull the head of an enemy king and who walked through life with this second head inside him stitched up with a golden thread. But on the day of Our Lord's Crucifixion observing the unusual darkness he called his Druid to ask what it omened, and the Druid Bacrach said that the Son of God was being crucified by the Jews, upon which the king with the head in his head got into an unholy dither, rushed at a grove and began hewing it with his sword to demonstrate how he would deal with those wicked Jews, and because of the excess of his fury the ball started from his head, his brain gushed out and in that way he died.

And did not the poet Edmund Spenser see an old foster mother drinking of the blood from the head of Murrough O'Brien at his execution in 1570 when Spenser's age was five and twenty. And were not the branches of the thorn trees an oddish red because they were stained in imitation of the precious blood of Christ, and the fuchsia flower called Deora Dia, or tears of Christ.

You are Irish you say lightly and behind you is all that plus the jargon about the proud melodious swans and the belling of the stag plus the tendency to be swamped in melancholy and loss.

Around you in a gaudy room covered with bits of ravelled carpet there are little pups piddling, there is an altar dedicated to Our Lady with points of artificial roses as sharp as thorns, and six small children – the occupants – looking at Shirley Temple on the television.

You have gone in for help and the driver is telling the woman what a bugger of a day it's been and he hopes he won't have to get a new engine. Orange juice is being consumed by the children and the father, a game man, says 'Say sorry' whenever a child burps. There isn't a hire car in the neighbourhood. Every driver is either gone to see relations in hospital or to evening Mass or 'went out and never came back'. This information is transmitted to you by the well-meaning woman as she makes condolences to the wife or mother or mother-in-law that she has been talking to on the phone.

Suddenly you must get away. Yes you wanted to come back but as time passes you feel they will pinion you down with their beliefs and their unyielding opinions. You read that the Countrywomen's Association favour bringing back the birch and a 'broadminded' person considers Ingmar Bergman's *Persona* as filth and pulp. Prick the religious sensibilities and underneath you will find Irish hearts on the boil. What would Yeats have to say now? – his literary revival gone to ashes with no phoenix peering through.

You are Irish you say lightly, and allocated to you are the tendencies to be wild, wanton, drunk, superstitious, unreliable, backward, toadying and prone to fits, whereas you know that in fact a whole entourage of ghosts resides in you, ghosts with whom the inner rapport is as frequent, as perplexing, as defiant as with any of the living. To meet one's kinsmen is to unleash a whole sea of unexpected emotionalism. I was having a walk one afternoon in London, and passing a building site I slowed down to shield my eyes from the likelihood of grit. A young Roscommon boy asked, 'Are you happy?'

'Not very,' I said.

He beamed at hearing a fellow-countrywoman.

'Any chance of tea at four?'

'No chance,' I said (I had to be somewhere).

'You won't forget us, will you?' he said.

'I won't,' I said.

Then I thought of another Roscommon man in a deserted pub one morning in Dublin, a madman by his own definition who had lodged there for years, along with two or three others, men in upstairs rooms with single trestle beds, feathers coming through the ticking of the pillow and the Sacred Heart somewhere or everywhere. 'Take that nice smile off your face,' he said to my son and was of mind to clout him for being so affable. He said, and his eyes were darting, that we were 'snottynoses' but that he knew the subject, predicate and object of any sentence. The woman behind the counter was having tea and aspirin and she shivered although she was wrapped in a variety of jumpers. He had whiskey and scorned us for having 'whayter'. The other lodger who had been there for ten or fifteen years was gone with his nerves. Upstairs in a window was a bullet mark and some scratches of bottled glass where a highwayman scratched his name on the window. Here too a table where Robert Emmet sat in the year 1800 and plotted a revolution that aborted into a mere scuffle. The table was stacked away with the past.

This is Godot land. The little pushbell with the 'house-maids only' sign no longer works and the cold corridors lead to locked rooms with cretonne over the glass-panelled doors to thwart peepers. At night during the tourist season there is a piano player and a fiddler and it is this, plus large rounds, plus thorny artificial tea roses and haunting love songs that the visitors are presented with, and not the cold rooms or the tiled landings or the old-fashioned lavatory with newspapers all over the pedestal, not the stone hot-water bottles or the men with shingles, and so it should be.

But when you are Irish you know both sides and you are curiously uneasy with both. Uneasy with the outsiders who expect their version of you to manifest – jolly witty roistering, even more uneasy with the natives who want you or anyone to lift them corporally out of their mire and desperation and bring them straight to heaven in a chariot. You are Irish you say lightly and you walk London streets at four and think of how Yeats predicted such a thing and walking the streets you have no trouble at all in re-invoking the wind that shakes the barley. When the sun does shine there it seems to sparkle with an extraordinary radiance, and this factor along with the lore about hospitality, fairies, pisrogues, geese put up a chimney to clean it, Yarra and Begorrah, have been abundantly written about, by good, bad and appalling writers. The handbooks say with an insouciance that handbooks are wizard at: 'There is a new prosperity everywhere and one can sense a feeling of optimism in the attitude of the people.' It goes on to talk about fashion, and elegance and heritage, and Joyce and Yeats and Behan (no living bard gets a laurel), and Christendom, and Nelson's pillar which, as it says, by being blown up in 1966 is 'evidence of the fierce emotions that have not completely died in the Irish people'. It omits to tell us that the stone head is deep down in the cellars of City Hall, wrapped up in an old sack, and that from the night he toppled he was first used by students to publicise a dance then smuggled to London and brought back by an antique dealer who enquired of the lunchtime crowd if anyone would buy it. A writer who would have devoted a day's rumination to that was Myles Na Gopaleen, sage, cogitator, and verbal leprechaun, a man who in his newspaper articles flayed the plain people of Ireland, consigning them to being turnip snaggers. In his novels this same man considered their more outlandish traits and made them into comic heroes.

But the writers and the poets always speak with a more natural feeling for a place and, if you want to feel Ireland's many guises you can feel it, say, in Somerville and Ross, a description of a day's hunt when 'frost and sunshine combined and went to one's head like iced champagne, and the hunting field (being) none other than long stretches of unfenced moorland and bog'. You get the showers of rain, the harriers in tumult, the riders, the onlookers in traps or bicycles or on foot, the lanes full of stones and furze bushes and the insurmountable stubborn grass banks. You read Frank O'Connor's description of a cycle through Cavan – blue lakes, little hills continuous and rolling, crabbed, stunted country which as he said 'was for a draughtsman and not a painter'. Uncloying country that produced in him a sense of gentle animation. J.M. Synge said he regretted every hour spent away from her and every night lived in a city. Elizabeth Bowen knew the landscape and mood of north-east Cork when in her story 'Summer Night' she wrote:

> Released from the glare of noon, the haycocks now seemed to float on the aftergrass: their freshness penetrated the air. In the not far distance hills with woods up their flanks lay in light like hills in another world – it would be a pleasure of heaven to stand up there, where no foot ever seemed to have trodden, on the spaces between the woods soft as powder dusted over with gold. Against those hills, the burning red rambler roses in cottage gardens along the roadside looked earthy – they were too near the eye. The road was in Ireland.

In a country so passionately dedicated to the banning of books it is amazing and maybe relevant that literature is still revered and any ploughman anywhere might recite to you about the 'Siege of Limerick', or the plight of wild geese, or those soldiers in their tents before the 'Battle of Fontenoy' invoking their native Clare:

> The whole night long we dream of you and waking think we're there.
> Brave dream and foolish waking we never shall see Clare.

That was my territory. A few miles from my birthplace was the seat of Brian Boru's former palace – Kincora – of which we used to chant 'Oh where, Kincora, is Brian the Great and where is the beauty that once was thine?' The road near there was dark and shielded by a dense vault of interlocking trees. There was a ball alley, green and lichened from saturations of rain, the trees rustled, the leaves rustled, and a man who lived in a nearby estate was a bird watcher and reputed to have always a fresh feather in his check hat. In the adjoining estate lived two ladies who did their own bottling and preserving, and both fortresses were flanked with great gates and ornamental limestone piers. Then inside were the low hunched fairy-story little gate-lodges with the windows diamond paned and the chimneys perpetually smoking. Driving there on one of those long-promised, never-to-be-forgotten, childhood outings we were told to look out for Kincora and suddenly a dizziness possessed me, seeing became impossible, what with the excitement, the speed of the car, what with the darkness, the ball alley. The eyes lost the power to focus and I missed seeing it. The car headed for Killaloe where we were going to see a bridge on which four local boys were shot, and a new houseboat owned by an Englishman. I thought of the poem, the beautiful lament that celebrated the place, and the poem became more a living thing than the actual bypassed landmark:

> *I am Mac Liag, and my home is on the lake.*
> *Thither often, to that palace whose beauty is fled,*
> *Came Brian to ask me, and I went for his sake*
> *Oh, my grief! That I should live, and Brian be dead!*

2 My home town

ORN AND BRED in a townland that bordered on other townlands of equal indistinctiveness. Fairly arable land, tillage in some fields, potatoes in most, potatoes sprayed twice a year and consequently the leaves bright as peacocks' plumage until the rain came and washed the copper sulphate away. During the summer one saw from any window the dock and the ragwort, rampant, high, and submerged in the grasses some old piece of rusted farm machinery and sometimes a fox making its way swiftly to the hen house. There were nice dozy hens, a sow, and to everyone's trepidation one reigning bull in some field or farmyard to which were brought all the resisting brown cows of the neighbourhood.

A bull had featured too in the mythology and had been the reason for a war. Queen Medb sat up in bed one night and found, upon comparing, that she and her husband had identical vessels, finger rings, clasps, diadems, flocks, swine, horses and wandering herds, but that there was a white bull in his keeping which had deserted from hers. This galled her. To amend she set out to acquire the Brown Bull of Cuailgne, and after some crooked bargaining a war ensued that was so wasteful, so bloody, so resulting in shame, dishonour and shambles, that one of her own tribe was forced to say they had followed 'the rump of a misguiding woman'. The word rump sent shivers through you, shivers of shame.

Life was fervid, enclosed and catastrophic. The spiritual food consisted of the crucified Christ. His Passion impinged on every thought, word, deed and omission, and sometimes in the wild fancifulness of childhood it was as if one caught sight of Him on a hill stretched out upon a Cross betwixt two thieves, with women at the foot of it, gnashing and weeping. His Passion had been deciphered for us from the shroud in which His Body lay. It was described how having been scourged He was then nailed to the Cross, one nail piercing both feet, His knees thrust out, His pectoral muscles corrugated and an overflow of blood and serum gushing from that Sacred Heart that had received the fatal spear stroke. As if that were not enough one learned of the blood flow that trailed sinuously across His forehead because of the crown woven of briar. One loved Him more than anything or anyone ever to take shape again. He loved one and at times spoke in an urgent whisper about the importance of being good. To be good was to be pure and yet the prayers had the glandular desperation ascribed to human love:

> King of virgins and lover of chastity and innocence, extinguish in my frame, by the dew of thy heavenly blessing, the fuel of evil concupiscence, that so an equal purity of soul and body may abide in me. Mortify in my members the lusts of the flesh and all harmful emotions, and give me true and persevering chastity with thine other gifts which please thee in truth, so that I may with chaste body and pure heart offer unto thee the sacrifice of praise. For with what contrition of heart and fountain of tears, with what reverence and awe, with what chastity of body and purity of soul, should that divine and heavenly sacrifice be celebrated, wherein thy flesh is indeed eaten, where thy blood is indeed drunk, wherein things lowest and highest, earthly and

divine, are united, where the holy angels are present, and where thou art in a marvellous and unspeakable manner both sacrifice and priest.

One kissed the huge prone cross on Good Friday and one felt the gravity of it and gazed at the gloomy altar bereft of flowers. One kissed one's mother's sallow cheek and thought of blancmange, now and then one secretively kissed a girl friend. A kiss was something dangerous that got born in the back of the throat, forming itself like a bud or a pearl, coming through the mouth and at last delivering itself on the lips which was in fact its shallowest manifestation. A face held all feeling, withheld what you felt about the others, but did not say, rather converted into a grimace or secretly stuck out your tongue when a back was turned. That was a sin, as almost everything was, and there would be retribution and maybe they would cut the tongue out of you with a black-bladed carving knife with which they cut soda bread and rashers, with which they decapitated the cockerel on Saturday morning in time for Sunday's lunch. The cockerel's body used to have the jitters long after its demise, used to dance all over the stone steps, where it would be placed for plucking beside the sewerage.

They were formidable people those adults with their inscrutable humours. Differing faces. Some with jowls, some with necks loose as turkeys' combs and some as unflinching as an ash plant. Not at all like the image of them propagated abroad, as being full of bluff and yarn and blarney. They were inclined to shout. Perhaps they had to fight the elements thus, the wind being such a feature, causing trees to blow down or slates to fly off the roof or great gusts of soot or nests to come scurrying down the chimney. These things were more manifest at night, these portents. Unde the covers for shelter, for safety you burrowed. Outside in the field the cows mooed, and kept each other company, lowing one to the other, sending sounds as fetching as a mother's across the air uniting one field with another, one herd with another.

Two or three days in the year were major events, and not many went by without rain or news of a funeral. The thrashing was an 'occasion' and the cottagers would come up into the yard with their asses and carts to get straw for bedding, straw for animals, straw for the pigs; while the bags of newly thrashed corn would be tied and stacked together, ready for the lorry to be sent to the mill to earn the money that was always bespoke anyhow. The workmen had to have three good meals regardless of the kind of harvest – often the barley was sodden with rain – and collations such as tea and loaf bread, besides. People helped. My father sent two of his men over to Mick the Master to save hay and they finding the Master on a binge, ran up a bill, with the butchers and the publican, treated themselves to afternoon naps in trams of hay, idled to such an extent and feasted that Mick the Master said, pointing in the approximate direction of the Lakeside Hotel, 'It would have been cheaper to dispatch them there.'

He had been Master of the Workhouse. When the Workhouse closed down it was let out to a carpenter and glazier, but the ex-Master with his big bushy dog and his walking cane was always addressed by his former title.

They move in and out of one's consciousness like summer bats. The poultry instructress who enjoined you again and again not to touch your teeth with your fork, the German engineer who came to help install the electricity, got short-taken on a bus, and kept saying 'pay-pay', which the conductor took to be that he wanted to pay again, whereas he wanted to jump off and get behind the nearest ditch. In the end he made his point by miming his desperately desired action.

There was a blacksmith with of course the black daubed face, who played the accordion and had a horde of tales. When he sang he sang through the nose affecting the style of some American crooner and his favourite rendering was a song called 'A Bunch of Violets', an ode concerning a rich lady, with a darling little daughter, who stopped to buy a bunch of pretty violets from a ragged little orphan she had spied. One thing led to another and the little boy was compelled to admit that everybody was loved by somebody, everybody had a father or a mother, a sister or a brother too, but that all the time, as long as he remembered, since he'd been a mite so

small, he seemed to be the only one that nobody loved at all. As fate and sen-
timent would have it he was the lady's long lost, deserted, illegitimate son.

The blacksmith was stopped on a street in Limerick by the film director
(Sean Aloysius) Ford during the making of *The Quiet Man.* John Ford
tapped him on the shoulder and is said to have said, 'You're the very man
I'm looking for.' The blacksmith naturally demurred, said he had no
acting ability, was dunce at everything except shoeing horses and lived
with his mother who wouldn't believe that such a thing could happen, and
John Ford is reputed to have said, ''Tis the eyes that count.' The
blacksmith also claimed to have seen Dorothy Paget in a dining room and
swore that she ate an entire chicken, bones and all.

There was a highly strung woman whose father had brandished a
Union Jack the day the Anglo-Irish treaty was signed and whose children
went mad periodically. There was a madman who lived in a hut, never
stirred out without his razor – cut-throat – which he took to sharpening on
any adjacent stone or step, saying he did not know but that he might meet
some devil whose throat he'd have to cut instantly. Always and in the
background the Devil himself horned and black, most often seen at night,
oftenest of all at dusk, and annually on stage a most bewitching
personification of him, in the person of Count Dracula, Count of Tran-
sylvania, who sucked the blood of maidens. You dreamed of going with
him, visualised the encounter backstage where he would at first rebuff you
and then be melted by your offers to pack his trunk, be his stand-in maiden
on whom he rehearsed the procedure of blood-sucking. Yes Dracula
and you would go away and you would revive the saintly side of him.

To be on an island makes you realise that it is going to be harder to
escape and that it will involve another birth, a further breach of waters.
Nevertheless an agitation to go.

Even local journeys were difficult, as transport was the great obstacle.
There were two bicycles, one a 'crock' which is to say there was always
something wrong with the tyres or the spokes or the pedals or the steering or
the handlebars themselves that were temperamental and wobbly.

sually one had to walk. It took half an hour to walk to the village and Easter Saturday that journey had all the joy of whatever is the opposite of pilgrimage, a feast after the rigours of fast and abstinence. On the last days of Lent local suffering reached its climax – they were holy hours, kissing of the Cross, further fasts, vigils in the chapel, with the statues and tabernacles draped in purple, all gaiety extinguished, the very flowers and flower vases taken away and continuous rounds of Stations in which the gaudy representations drew attention to His fall, His scourge, the small tenderness afforded him by Veronica who offered Him a hand towel, the lamentation of His mother and His being nailed to a Cross upon which He died. But on the Saturday there was a feeling of relief and exultation, all pain and humiliation over, at least for a while, and as it were the little lambs frisking in the fields, simnel cake, almond iced, the Easter water and an orgy of plain and milk chocolate after seven long weeks of deprivation.

'Oh God whose praise and martyred innocence did this day proclaim, not by speaking but by dying, do to death in us all the malice of sinfulness that our lives may also proclaim thy faith which our tongues profess.' So we prayed.

On Easter Sunday morning itself, further rapture – bright vestments, heavenly food, optimism, the very same as if one could go home to a private resurrection.

A spinster suffering from rheumatics gave piano lessons and had a little rusty rod for hitting knuckles with. She preferred a brown egg to a white egg, and bought two at a time. She lived with a sister, and later alone. How did they survive it – those long years, from meal to meal, from Sunday to Sunday, their lives as static as the aspidistra in the occasional first-floor middle window.

Nurses in love with doctors, and the new teacher in love with a bachelor from up the country to whose house she had never been. He courted her in her digs which is to say he sat in the folding chair (got from cigarette coupons) opposite her, and smoked until it was time to have tea, play cards and go home. She had her landlady primed to ask the key questions:

Landlady:　How many fireplaces are in your house now, Sean?
Sean:　What do you want to know for?
Landlady:　We need to know how many firescreens to accept as
　　　　　wedding presents.
Sean:　Ah sure, a furze bush will do.

The teacher died young, in the hospital named after St Jude the patron of
hopeless cases, and one hour before, held up her hands, displayed her thin
wrists and said, 'I'll have to get all new style when I come out of here.' She
is remembered for having introduced piped icing, little scalloped roses and
carageen soufflés, into a bastion doggedly committed to potatoes and bacon
and cabbage.

　　Men who were courting used to wait on the roadside and let out their
low signalling whistles. Courtships were desperate affairs conducted in
bogs and mires, eked out in the secrecy of wet hedges. And were they
inarticulate affairs apart from the body's noises, apart from the grunts?

　　The sinless pleasures were eating, drinking, the carnival, the mission,
and the races. At the races were the 'law-di-daws' with cards and
binoculars, the bookies with easels and blackboards, tick-tack men, and
the bulks of people trooping around asking each other if they had had the
winner. Mostly the men did the betting and the women and children converged in the stalls and booths where the vendors sold powdered lemonade, oranges, bone bangles, and where china dogs were put up for raffle.

　　At night the amusements started up and the place was a mecca with
multi-coloured strings of light, fairy bulbs going twinkle-twinkle, and
every conceivable distraction such as bumper cars in which people could
sit and bump blazes out of their friends and enemies. There were swing
boats too, and a big dipper full of screaming people revolving around in
order to get a thrill. You heard it but did not see it. The opportunity never
came. It was always to be next year but by the next year there was still not a
seat to spare in the hackney car. You would marvel at hearing of a man
who ate razor blades without doing a bit of damage to his tongue or his

gullet. Inwardly you would conclude that he was a freak and not constituted like Mary who swallowed her own little watch and had to take castor oil 'to pass the time away'.

Those who dealt in bangles, doilies and carnival glass were hawkers, self-styled gypsies, who dashed about in their sidecars from town to town whipping the horses if ever they lagged. Your mother did not trust them, said they would be up to any mischief, any theft, said God knows whose fender or coal scuttle lurked under their faded tartan rugs. Your father described how one autumn one of those tawny ladies went down to the orchard, bought the apples off the trees, picked them with her own hands, wrapped them in twists of paper and kept them in perfect condition for a race day the following spring. Those apples, he claimed, were the best in the world, vivid red skins on them and even the flesh with a ripple of red running through it like a dye. The orchard was in ruin, trees diseased and bent over, nettles clambering between the piles of rubbish dumped over the years. The last old bachelor was not equal to keeping it up.

He would soon die.

Dying was often preceded by a death knock or something more incriminating. The night before the keeper in the gate-lodge died, a frog had leapt out of the ashes and likewise when his wife died, and their daughter long before. They were addicted to wintergreen, oil of eucalyptus, and griddled bread. The iron marks of the griddle would brand the pale surface of the warm bread. You accompanied your mother and it was like going to a distant land, although it was only a hundred yards down the lawn and out the gateway, and into the little fairytale cottage, with its rambling roses and smell of clay because of the flower beds being flush up to the whitewashed wall. You would be given griddled bread and biscuits with tiny holes in them through which the jam could be made to trickle, jam or better still, jelly.

The gatekeeper and his wife shared the same rimless spectacles got from a travelling man, 'the Jew man' who came twice a year with his canteen of spectacles and the little buff-coloured serrated cloth for polishing with. The

city of Limerick and the eye specialist were twenty Irish miles
anything such as spectacles to be changed or a wet battery to be re
had to be sent in by bus. The obliging conductor spent his entire day
city doing everyone's errands. My father was waiting down at the lodge
send his own horn-rimmed glasses to Limerick for repair – he had sat on
them – and hearing the bus come, he ran out, but picked up the Wattle
spectacles by mistake and as a result neither of them could read the paper for
a week. When restored the lenses were found to be thick and blotchy,
giving them both blinding headaches. A coolness ensued between the two
families.

The dead people looked different, they looked paler, insouciant, drained
of all their fret and agitation. Young or old, the dead faces had something of
the mild beauty of a narcissus, but they smelt dead and the tears that were
shed were because they were dead, and the clay pipes and the rosaries and
the barrels of porter consumed, and the big glass hearse, and the candles,
and the linen cloths, were all to denote the mournful event, that would last
throughout eternity.

There was one person who was not white at all but red and hacked
about, and bits of his flesh strewn, and his poor body mixed up with
machinery because he had driven into a telegraph pole, in his car. The
thud brought the people out of their houses, each one asking 'what, what?',
until someone brought a lantern, and people didn't know what they were
likely to confront, and my father said he thought the dying creature had
tried to make an act of contrition, although beheaded. He was bundled up
somehow, and buried, and had a hurley field named after him and up at
home along with a souvenir of him – a chrome door handle – there was
framed and on display a letter to a mother describing a son's death, equally
gory, but presumably the will of God. I used to cry over it, be frightened,
and in the end tried to fathom it:

Great though the burden of your sorrow I feel it will to some extent be
lightened by the thought that your dear one received all the ministrations of

Holy Religion and as a result died a very holy and happy death. In response to an urgent call I reached his side on the river bank about twenty minutes after the fatal accident. He was still quite conscious and despite his shocking injuries was externally very calm and self-possessed. He made his confession with mature deliverance (making at the same time a short review of his whole life) and repeated the act of contrition and all the other prayers with an earnestness and fortitude which seemed to make him oblivious of all pain. At the same time he received Extreme Unction and Last Blessing but for a certain reason not Holy Viaticum. I was very anxious that he should not be deprived of that privilege, and so when he had been removed to the hospital, some hours later I saw him again. I had another long talk with him on spiritual matters, found him still fully recollected and to my great delight, found I could administer Holy Viaticum. It was a supreme pleasure, too, for him to know he could at last receive his Lord. I assisted him in making his thanksgiving and knowing he had then but very few hours to live the sad duty devolved on me of practically telling him so. I then asked if he had any final messages for his friends. He simply said, 'Tell my mother I am dying happy. Tell her not to worry but pray for me, say goodbye to her and father, we shall all meet soon again.' I then took final leave of the poor fellow telling him I would see him again later in the evening. When I called again he was under the influence of morphine so I gave him again the Last Blessing and departed, I must say with a very heavy heart, and with deep resentment in my heart towards the perverted minds of men who invent death traps in the shapes of bombs to mutilate and mar the beauty of God's masterpieces; brave men. I may tell you in conclusion that everything humanly possible was done by doctors, sisters and the National Army and that his death was made as easy and peaceable as it could be in the sad circumstances – clergy and laity of the town showed their sympathy with him and his dear comrade in an unmistakable manner. Yet I know not all these things can eliminate the sorrow of a mother's broken heart. You must only think of that other mother who too gazed on the mangled body of her dear son. May she, the mother of sorrows, comfort you so in your great sorrow is my earnest prayer.

Yours,
Father so-and so

P.S. I did not convey to you in my hurried note your dear boy's final moments, also when his uniform had been removed the night nurse found some notes and wondered what she should do with them. He simply said 'Have masses said for both of us' – intimating his comrade Lieut. Flynn. Though under the influence of morphine – poor fellow – he remained conscious to the end and repeated the act of contrition and pronounced the holy name a few moments before he passed away. All things considered, therefore, you can appreciate what a beautiful death your boy had. He certainly is with God. Good though he was and the idol of your heart he is not too far from God.

The eight neighbouring Protestants would never reach that destination and neither would the black doctor or the travelling Jew man. In fact the black doctor reached the county jail after a farmer had died having his teeth extracted by pincers and the newspapers said, DOCTOR JAILED FOR EXTRACTING MOLARS FROM THE MOUTH OF MULLIGAN. The Jew man went into the dispensary and was asked for a urine specimen and refused to give it saying he would bring it the following week. Task performed, he had to wait another week for results and upon hearing the good news telephoned his wife who was a carpetbagger in Belfast and said 'You're all right, I'm all right and little Noah's all right.' To get value for money he had mixed the urines, blended them. Urine stories were sauciest, especially the one about the parish priest who, suspecting that his housekeeper was helping herself to his sherry, decided to dilute it with urine, and after weeks of this and still the level in the decanter flagrantly going down, he tackled her about it and she said, 'Oh Father, I put a drop in your soup every day.'

Nothing went unknown or unjudged. Mick the Master's housekeeper was told never to serve anything, not even a cup of tea, without serving it on a tray. One day, for the benefit of guests, when asked to show the kittens she brought in six kittens bunched up on the silver gallery tray. The girl from up the country using the telephone for the first time, thought that, as with a wire, economy was vital and picking up the dreaded instrument she spoke to her brother in London and said, 'Come quick, Jim sick, Babbie.' Ever after she was called not by her real name, but Jim-Sick Babbie.

The Jew man was shunned as were the gypsies and the hawkers, all bringing upon themselves unvoiced odium, which was mysteriously connected with sex and connected with the fact that they had sallow skin and quivering nostrils. Furriers were Jews, jewellers were Jews, and they were not above taking the precious jewels out of your watch or the best strips of fur and replacing with counterfeit. There had been a pogrom in Limerick half a century before and a redemptorist priest told the faithful to stone the moneylenders which they did.

Limerick was an exemplary city. Everyone flocked to confraternities. The friars in their brown robes and sandals moved through the city doing the corporal works of mercy. At the side door of the friary there would be a huddle of people, some who had come to beg for bread and soup, others waiting to hand in their offerings to have masses said for their departed. At ten or eleven years, when on a visit, you sat in a chapel with your legs crossed and were asked by an incensed lady to please uncross them at once. 'Did you not know,' she said, 'that Our Lady blushes whenever a woman does such an indecent thing.'

LIMERICK: *City of churches and beautiful spires.*
City of pubs and lowly desires.
City of gossips that tell what they're told.
City of youth that waits to grow old.
Society's city the home of the snob.
Show me your penny before you hob-nob.
Do have a coffee do have a bun.
Do what the others do 'cos it is done.

At school we were told that in 1690 during the siege of Limerick the seventeen gates were shut, the inhabitants defending themselves with sticks and stones, even the women pouring boiling stirabout on the English soldiers' heads. Then how the Grenadiers leaped forward with their

My father, Michael O'Brien

A gambler. Your father said mice could be stopped in their tracks, mystified, by putting salt on their tails and he tried it and when it didn't paralyse them, he flung shoes, a last, every conceivable object. The doctor and he took bets as to who would make the first slaughter. They were exhilarated by it. The mice went clambering up the walls in desperate attempts to escape the various peltings. The saltcellar got emptied. A dying mouse let out a last and unbecoming screech and he asked your mother to loan him a tanner so that he could honour his debt. He was livid at having lost.

The boys won't leave the girls alone
They tossed my hair and broke my comb . . .

A County Clare farmer

'I saw Hickey coming over the field and I waved to him.
He was driving the cows. They straggled across the field,
stopping for a minute, as cows will, to stare idly at nothing.
Hickey was whistling and the evening being calm
and gentle his song went out across the field. A stranger
going the road might have thought it was a happy place.'

PREVIOUS PAGES

Cottages on the Aran Islands

J. M. Synge considered the Aran Islands the most primitive part left in Europe. He brought a camera there and along with writing his *Aran Notebooks*, he photographed the girls whose long lashes lent a shade to their wistful eyes. He thought the red petticoats they wore surmounted by deep blue shawls more quietly fair than any peasant costume he had met with in Europe. But he thought too that without this red relief the island would be a nightmare fit to drive one to murder in order to gloat awhile on the fresh red glow of blood. Yeats said of him that he had a furious impartiality and an indifferent turbulent sorrow.

Curraghs preparing to row out to the steamer. The Atlantic.

The Curraghs come into the isle of Ireland with turf from Connemara and provisions from Galway. The inhabitants sit along the sea wall and watch with astonishing patience everything that is going on, that has gone on, and will go on, until perhaps the end of time.

grenades but how the Irish replied with a discharge of shot 'as fast as t'was possible'. By the time the gates were shut for the night five hundred Englishmen were lost upon the spot and a thousand more were wounded! Next day King William trained his forty guns on the inadequate fortifications. Hot balls of fire projected into the bloodied streets, people collapsed, horses collapsed, while the civilians went on toiling to extinguish the flames. After seventeen days of similar combat a wall was bridged and the Grenadiers in their piebald yellow and red, with furred headgear, and bells jangling from their belts, went in with hand grenades. However, they suffered an immediate check and all over that soft and lazy land watered by the River Shannon was the crackle of musket fire, explosion and thick columns of smoke.

Courage mounted. Those who were merely onlookers at first, civilians living on raw beans and raw oats, entered into the fray to put new spirit into the exhausted Irish. The English were driven back, inch by inch, and finally to their very own camp in ignominy and shame.

The rain came – the soft and faithful rain of Ireland, washing the blood-splashed streets and handicapping the Williamites by making their camp site into a marsh. The waters of the Shannon were rising, the English soldiers were up to their knees in mud, and dysentery was rife.

King William fled and all was augured for an Irish victory but such a thing did not happen because Patrick Sarsfield, the leader, was deserted because of jealousy by his colleague Tyrconnell, who sailed for France, taking with him the French forces and the best of the artillery. Dissension broke out, the soldiers and the civilians were at loggerheads and by the following year after a siege lasting six weeks, with terrible privation and terrible bombardments, Sarsfield himself capitulated and pressed for a treaty.

The Irish were so often on the verge of the victorious, when fate, a fresh enemy, bungling, weariness, or inner treachery altered events. So we were told in the classroom day after day, year after year, and so subconsciously we developed our notions of destiny and all its vicissitudes.

Kitchen garden

The gardens of the big estates are jumbled and beautiful. Here, shrubs, flowers and mossy trees fight one another for light and survival while at dawn and again at dusk the rooks start up their inexorable din. The gardens dishevelled though they are, survive as remnants of the ruined and burnt house.

3 The classroom

CLASSROOM WINDOWS were high, with small panes that were seldom cleaned. The unreachable catch was broken so that the window had to be forced open with a crook and held ajar with a can or a scrubbing brush or whatever was to hand. Some days this proved the impossible and the room became stuffy. A long room. First thing in the morning water sprinkled from a cup, along the floor, prior to sweeping. Then the onslaught of information. It was there that one devoured history, it was there that the whole of the rest of the country came into being simply by looking at the grey shredding cloth map, with its little spots of red to denote capital towns and zig-zags to trace the course of the rivers. It was there one heard of the Giant's Causeway and from a little brown book heard in Irish and in English the names of local townlands, names designated because of their characteristics:

The Turnip Growing Hillside
The Hill Abounding in Ivy
The Hump
The Mouse's Meadow
The White Island
The Pleasant Island
The Sorrell Island
The Hill Covered with
    White Thorn Bushes

The Hill of Counsel
The Hill of the Little Declivity
The Snipes' Booly
The O'Brien's Booly
The Old Stronghold
The Monks' Land
The Birdless District
The Two Paps of Danann

The powder for making ink came from the city, and the big winchester for holding it had little air bubbles in the interior of the green glass. It was a hazardous operation mixing ink, and there was spilt stuff in weird stains all over the floor, stains incurred on different occasions but there forever. There were holes in the floor down which the mice scurried, and some girls said they had seen rats. The big important dictionary needed the strength of two girls to get it out of the press. Each letter was indexed in black, in the shape of a thumb, on the margin so that a word could be looked up in a jiffy. We learned that 'intenerate' softens or makes tender and that 'fear intenerates the heart making it fit for all gracious impression'. Also that 'empidae' were not akin to gnats but flew in numbers over water on summer evenings and lived partly on other insects and on the juice of flowers. Everyone scratched themselves on hearing that. One would suddenly be asked the meaning of a word, a difficult word and, as the lady teacher said, one never came up to expectations, one failed, missed, miscarried, disappointed. Then she would point to the leather-bound dictionary and say 'Forage, forage' and for no reason would faithfully recite:

> In the lexicon of youth which faith reserves
> For a bright manhood, there is no such word as failed.

Then a lady came to teach step dancing on Thursdays, tried to initiate us into the mystery of jigs and reels. There being no musical accompaniment, we were all asked to hum. Lovely firm calves to her legs, dark stockings and shoes with a beautiful strap up the length of the instep. The humming varied. Some girls spoke. 'One two three four five six seven, all good children go to heaven, when they die their sins are forgiven, one two three four five six seven.' A lesson cost a penny. A few girls took the class while the others sat at their desk pretending to study, re-reading all about the Battle of Kinsale or a description of a crisp morning in New England as described by Thoreau. It was beyond our means so I was pleased, although embarrassed to sit aside and not be able to partake, and in my heart of hearts I was eternally grateful, believing as I did that dancing disturbed the body and might in an extremity drive all the fluids and bloods and entrails out of one. The dancing mistress was in love and that covered a multitude. Love was the embrocation for everything, love would do miracles.

The teacher who was highly strung let implements fly from time to time – pens, pencils, pencil cases, set squares, caps, books and a medley of language that was a compote of Irish, English, Latin and raillery. Then the next day, or the day following, she would atone by letting us read, by letting the infants mix all the new plasticine so that it was streaked and multi-coloured, and she would bring toffees or the remains of an iced cake and pass it around on a cake plate to be shared. That of course created a fresh anxiety because one never knew if it would get to one, or worse still if it would get to the girl just before, and one could almost taste the icing and see the crumbs on her lips. Once the teacher made a little jam omelette for herself, on the open fire and gave half to a girl who was on her way to the closets. Boys' closets and girls'. Rough wood. Buckets. Poor sanitation. So the vaccinating doctor said the day he came with his lady nurse beside him. Her task was to put the swabs of iodine on the appointed spot and hold the jerking arm until he prodded it, then jabbed, then said 'next please'. The lady nurse went down to the closets and stayed there for an age and afterwards the floors – all three tiled floors – and the main murky passageway were running with blood, a veritable river of it. Why was that? What had happened?

In the evening the doctor and his escort – paler now – drove off, back to the capital where the streets were so narrow it was said that people could shake hands from their upstairs windows, the capital famous for having seen the presence not to mention the oratory of the quivering Daniel O'Connor and the austere De Valera.

When it rained and the yard was too wet for playtime, we huddled in the porch – forty or fifty girls – like hens except that we were chattering, huddled next to the reek of turf. Turf can get into one's head, making thoughts brown and sodden and flaky as the stuff itself. We would eat lunch there. Everyone's lunch much the same – thick slices of bread and butter, with sugar sprinkled on some, and a little bottle of water or milk. Our coats would be on hooks, coats slung on top of one another all threatening to fall off, then pixie caps of multifarious orders, scarfs and wool gloves that had been chewed and re-chewed and were anything but pristine.

Your best jumper was from a prize pattern, little diamonds of colour, zig-zags, the cynosure of all. You were called in by your teacher on an important occasion for it to be inspected by someone. By whom? You have forgotten. Forgotten everything except the beautiful waves of colour, and the zip with the flecked tassle at the end, and the ribbed cuffs of navy wool, that doubled over twice in case you should grow. You wore it Sundays, Holy Days and the days inspectors came. You told the catechism inspector that after the miracle of the loaves and fishes, when all had eaten to their satisfaction, Christ asked them to gather up the remains and that proved that He was not partial to waste.

The fishes in your imagination were flesh pink, medium sized like dab, and the loaves were white like altar breads, only fatter and spongier. The place where the miracle occurred was green and leafy and not at all the sparse sanded land that you were later to see. After the inspector went you all got a telling off, were told you could sweep the countryside with your brains except that instead you all chose to be bostoons. The only girls who did not get a telling off were the ones who were permanently dense and from whom nothing was expected beyond the norm. On that day they were the proud ones with their arms folded, and something verging on compliments descending on them because of the neatness of their appearance, or because they knew when to close the door or put a sod on the fire.

It was all very unpredictable. The teacher could flare up, have fits, pet some girls on the backs of their knees, have sets on other girls, then mysteriously change her mind and applaud those whom she was previously denigrating. But when the boy's master got into a tear it was bedlam for everyone. He roared and shouted and any adjacent boy was in danger of having his brains bashed out, onto the desk. He could be heard a mile away, roaring at whatever unfortunate boy was his butt. It was a constant threat like living close to Mount Vesuvius. His wife prayed, said constant ejaculations, and told women on the way down from Mass that he had not realised his ambition. He did the crosswords, had greyhounds that were fidgety and as a consequence the woodwork in their rambling house had the teeth marks of baying dissatisfied dogs.

Monday mornings were especially tense – compositions were handed over or not handed over, lies were told, how a mother or a father had been taken sick and how the fire was in no mind to light not having been lit for two whole days. The compositions were usually about 'A Day in the Life of a Penny' or 'A Day in the Life of a King' or 'A Day in the Life of a Bee' and we had to do lessons while she sat down to correct them and laughed outrageously at the clumsiness of our thoughts and our ideas. With a ruler as a pointer one girl would trace the course of the river, most often the River Shannon, with its important tributary, the Suck, and in the corner of our eyes we imagined the mice's tails as they curled above the level of the holes, or stared at the jam jars of lilac that had been brought in by one of the country girls and had withered on the window ledge so that specks of petal were lying like bits of must there and the water in the jar would have gone off.

But another world altogether prevailed – one of arms, crests, spears,

Lughaidh Laeighseach, son of Laeigh, son of the renowned Conall Cearnach, chief of the Red Branch Knights of Ulster, unbecomingly slain by a tribe which was later brutally avenged. Or a poem about Owen Roe O'Neill, 'Him they poisoned whom they feared to meet with steel', or a description of Shane O'Neill's body dug up at Carrickfergus, the head cut off and dispatched to Dublin where it was exhibited on the castle battlements. Shane O'Neill was a tough man because upon being told that they had murdered his only son he had replied that he had many sons. These daily inculcations of history, so immediate, so heart-rending and so riveting that it was possible to conceive of Sarsfield, Shane O'Neill and Bold Robert Emmet, and Sarah Curran his sweetheart as characters who might step out of the pages and into the room. All had sacrificed themselves for the Cause, and each had failed – one went into lowly exile, the other had his head on the castle battlement, the third was executed in the Liberties and made a speech from the dock that wrung our hearts – how his blood was not congealed by artificial terrors, and that though the lamp of his life was nearly extinguished he was ready to die and asked only for the charity of silence until such time as his country was free and not annexed to England.

Fair Sarah Curran went abroad, married and of course died of a broken heart. To Theobald Wolfe Tone, too, honour cursed with defeat. In 1796 with a hundred guineas in his pocket he went to Paris to secure a large force to help overthrow the British government in Ireland. The Bantry Bay expedition was the result of that, and Tone sailed for Ireland with an army of fifteen thousand men under the command of General Hoche and General Grouchy. His account of that voyage was like a letter from a son to each one of us.

> The wind is still high, and as usual right ahead; and I dread a visit from the English; and altogether I am in great uneasiness. Oh, that we were once ashore, let what might ensue after; I am sick to the very soul of this suspense. . . . We are here, sixteen sail, great and small, scattered up and down in a noble bay, and so dispersed that the enemy are now so close that if it blows

tonight as it did last night they will inevitably run foul of each other, unless one of them prefers driving on the shore.

Then the bitter tail-piece – three ships sunk, the others parted from each other, a difference of opinion with Grouchy and such storms as made Tone fear that it was his fate to submit and turn back to France. Two years later he led another fleet which was dismantled, captured by the British and led into Lough Swilly. Tone was taken prisoner. As the gallows was being erected outside his window, he cut his throat with a penknife but did not die at once and said to the surgeon that it was a pity he had been such a bad anatomist.

One had only to look out the long window and see the masts, the rigging, the ribs, the rudders and the sails appearing over the bottle-topped walls. The sea was forty miles away and, as we were told, withheld at one side by shining sheer gigantic black cliffs, from whence a priest was sucked in one afternoon, while doing a spot of fishing. Conjecture as to whether he could have given himself absolution or even uttered an act of contrition as he hurtled forward and downwards in the wake of the bamboo fishing rod that he'd bought in the hardware shop the day before. The sea spelt catastrophe but then all waters did, even the lordly Shannon into which cars had driven, or boats were overturned or men delivered up their own lives. The Shannon lake shone in summer and was hazed over with a special fly in the month of May, a fly for fishing with, for dapping. Lough Dearg Deirc – the Lake of the King of the Red Eye, so named because an unreasonable grasping bard had asked the King of Thomand for an eye, whereupon the King plucked out his own, gave it over, went down to the lake to wash, but his socket bled until the lake was not water but human blood.

Another of our heroes was Patrick Sarsfield, Lord of Lucan, who upheld the cause of the Catholics and of James II during the Jacobite war in Ireland. A photograph taken of his portrait showed him wearing a ringleted wig, a coat of armour and a white lace cravat worn French style.

The teacher would pound the floor with her cane and recite:

> *Farewell Oh Patrick Sarsfield*
> *May luck be on your path*
> *Your camp is broken up*
> *Your work is marred for years!*

We would be told again and yet again of how Sarsfield stole out of Limerick City one night with Galloping Hogan, a brave rapparee, and an army of men to intercept the train that was bringing ammunition to the Williamites who were laying siege to the city. Luck attended that night ride. There was no moon, the horses' hooves were muted, Hogan knew the back roads and the byroads and one of the soldiers met up with a prattling woman, wife of a Williamite who was able to give the password, 'Sarsfield is the word and Sarsfield is the man'. They got through the enemy lines, blew up eighteen wagons of train and ammunition, and the environs were such in that part of the country that the earth was rent. Sarsfield was the ring-leader but the name of Galloping Hogan had to be celebrated too because as a rapparee, he was one of that band of men who fought with pikes and scythes and muskets, who hid in hills until nightfall, who lay like otters in the water, but were swift as the mountain mist, and no small matter of mesmerisation to the enemy. But Patrick Sarsfield became a 'wild goose'. We would look up to the sky and think of flight and if that was not enough we would read:

> And now alas the saddest day is come that ever appeared above the horizon of Ireland. The sun was darkened, and covered over with a black cloud as if unwilling to behold such a woeful spectacle; there needed no rain to bedew the earth, for the tears of the disconsolate Irish did abundantly moisten their native soil to which they were at that day to bid their last farewells. Those who resolved to leave it never hoped to see it again and those who made the unfortunate choice to continue therein, could at the same time have nothing in prospect but contempt and poverty, chains and imprisonment and in a word all the miseries that a conquered nation could rationally expect from power and malice.

That was only fiddlesticks as she said compared with the accounts of the famine, the air as John Mitchell had written calm and pall-like, a vast silence, a creeping ruin over everything, an inability to curse because human passion had been quelled through starvation; children's eyes were senseless and wizened, work gangs who built walls and roads were voiceless like shadows, womanhood had ceased to be womanly, the birds carolled no more, the ravens dropped dead on the wing, and dogs hairless and with their vertebrae like the saw of a bone slunk into the ditch like wolves and the *anima mundi*, the soul of the land, was dim dying and dead. A world where help and pity did not forthcome.

The Justice of the Peace at Cork had written to the Duke of Wellington to tell how he took as much bread as five men could carry to a certain hamlet, and thought they were all dead, but upon going into a hovel realised by the low moaning that they were alive, two hundred phantoms or so most of whom were delirious. A woman who had just given birth tore his neck collar from him, another woman was seen to drag out the corpse of her child, a girl of twelve, and leave it half-covered with stones. Seven wretches lay huddled under the same cloak but though one of them was dead the others seemed not to notice or not to care. He asked the Duke to go to the young and gracious Queen, to appeal to her to use authority, in short to let the Irish eat some of the corn that grew in abundance that year. He implored that the frigid and flimsy chain of official etiquette be broken and that the Duke go directly to her. It was a letter sent in vain and the appeal was not met. Some survived on such things as nettles, chickweed or sorrel and those who could tottered along to the stockyards across the country in the hope of being able to procure a portion of blood taken from heifers or bullocks. The remainder set sail for America and must constitute the bulk of the forty million of Irish extraction in that land today.

The following year the Queen visited Ireland and thought that everything went off beautifully and when she stepped ashore at Cove, County Cork, the enthusiasm was immense. It is probable that the people were too debilitated to be anything else and yet they surpassed themselves according to her, by becoming noisy and jumping and shrieking.

The same grinding themes then – victimisation, misapprehension, aborted revolutions, informers, chaos and bungle, misheard instructions in the heat of battle, and half-drilled peasants mistakenly flinging away their arms and even their coats begging for quarter in some bog before being put to the sword. Then one girl – the doctor's daughter who had a watch – would hold it up so that the teacher could see, and then it would be time to go, and we would already have started up, like a herd, while the blackened bell went 'cling clang cling clang'. We would leave behind us oak desks littered with books and jotters and a teacher suddenly quiet, opaque, staring, possibly wondering what she might do for the remainder of the day without the annoyance and the companionship of us.

Out the door. An immediate vista of hawthorn bushes, then four tumbledown cottages complete with half doors, and directly opposite the doctor's house with its cross dog called Spot. To gain admission a youngster had to go to the back door, and that entailed going through a narrow enclosed passage in which one was incarcerated with Spot to the jeers of two or three of one's pals. Spot would grind his teeth, as if having a little rehearsal of them, then bare them so that one had a view of them along with the tongue that ranged in colour from fawn to a pale blubbery pink. You knew it was a question of tactics, not walking too fast, pulling the hem of your coat down so that it almost met the top of your new socks, so that no skin was bared to tempt him, carrying but not brandishing a twig, careful to convey no menace. He would have the tail of the coat, and you would be screaming when at that moment one or other of the occupants would come out and in a theatrical manner would bow and invite you to step inside.

Inside there was a stove comparable with no other in that neigh-bourhood, enamel no less, and the colour of the clouds when they were not quite blue and not quite grey; a stove, a grandfather clock and cutlery on the table for a two-course dinner, the main dish and a sweet. You were given pandy. The butter was yellow and floating in a crevice on the top and you swallowed the stuff down without chewing in order to get to the sago or the semolina or the steamed pudding. Steamed puddings were the most inviting of all particularly when tipped out of their bowl and turned upside down so that a cape of melted jam flowed over the top and down the ridges like a stream covering a stone. The anticipation of joy gave you the jitters. Everything swayed, and your eyes and the walls had a different rapport with each other so that the paper or the glossy paint came away from the wall in blisters.

On the way home a lady would tap the shop window with her knitting needle and ask some pointless question such as 'How is your mother', or 'How is your father'. A fat woman in a basket chair with heaving bosom and raspberry brooch pinned to the middle, would tell you to please pass on, pass on, because you were obstructing the sun, and a man with a yen for pedantry would digress on the clemency or the inclemency of the weather, as the case may be, on the toxic odours as a result of a pig fair, on the preponderance of matters of the heart and the occultation of feeling (I think he loved my mother).

But most of the other men were unknown and identified by their big boots and their snortles and their ash plants and the awe they engendered. They were just names – the father of such and such a girl or the owner of such a mowing machine or the master of such and such a dog. They all had nicknames, and they all had hidden desires. One man used to hide behind hedges lying in wait for girls, curling his forefinger, curling the tip of his tongue, opening his fly and oftener than not dragging some unfortunate girl in there. At least so went the rumour. It was on a lonely road, on the way to the graveyard, a road you seldom took, except in a funeral procession. Sometimes, in the town, you would buy a penny or a half-penny worth of sweets, rainbow toffees, or Fox's mints, or scorched almonds, and you would suck each one slowly, and your passage through the town on the way home from school would be at once slow and furtive, gawking at windows, waiting for a surprise, waiting for Christmas – always waiting for Christmas. Christmas was that glittering spray of tinsel down the two sides of the drapery window, a slip or a nightgown with a coloured ball on it, and the wide white meshed stocking enclosing a hoard of secret delights. Christmas was that, and a turnip with a lighted candle in it, lest Christ would pass your way and want to come in. Christmas was three Masses in one day and a Christmas dinner, and long before – but you did not know it – Christmas for James Joyce was the plum pudding and the brandy butter, and the happiness of a dinner table disrupted because one woman was religious and raged against Parnell the adulterer, taking issue with a guest.

Past the yellow town hall where twice a year the players came, where on occasion there were supper dances, and on Sunday night fourpenny hops where girls were liable to get into trouble; over the stone bridge where the water with the brownness of gushing porter washed the boulders and rinsed the hotel window and behind that window in the dark kitchen, men drank porter and three 'fast ladies' – one of whom had an Eton crop – drank gin and it and once under the influence were 'mad for mate'.

And even on the best of days with the sun shining, the leaves in a beautiful harmonious sway, the bees buzzing, the cattle drinking down by the waterside, a sort of terror lurked. Might the men undo their breeches, especially the man on the dole who made a speciality of it and who dragged girls into swamps where they became helpless. Or might not tinkers take one and sell one at a horse fair to strangers. Or the hermaphrodite might cross your path sitting astride her big cart and causing your flesh first to go creepy and then to be completely turned inside out as if being disembowelled. Only the women were safe to pass and even they might tirade about something you could not understand such as that milk had gone sour or a cow had given birth to a stillborn calf. There were mad women too who flounced about, tossed kerchiefs and said 'no, no' when their brothers or their keepers put harnesses on them to drag them to the lunatic asylum. Only mothers were safe to be with.

Mothers were best. Mothers worked and worried and sacrificed and had the smallest amount on their plates when the family sat down to eat, mothers wore aprons and slaved and mothers went to the confraternity on a Sunday evening and whispered things to each other in the chapel grounds about their wombs and their woes. A woman that was always going to her husband's grave would take your hand, shake it fiercely, whereupon the water would start up in her cataracted eyes.

Mothers never sat under willow trees or on rugs organising picnics, handing out savouries from a delicious basket. Mothers never hummed or did the highland fling. One mother had an operation and her husband was let in to gaze upon her asleep and naked upon the table. That was scandalous that was. But they were Protestants. That mother recovered, and made her own ice cream, raspberry flavoured, a lovely moist inviting shell of red. She had a house-maid.

Maids were all alike, streelish, always from the mountains, maids stopped going to school at eleven or twelve, could not read or write, had loads of brothers and sisters, were kleptomaniacs, had ladders in their stockings, and always ate when their mistresses were out. As a punishment they got locked in attics and lumber rooms where they bawled and yelled until they were eventually let out but had to go without supper and were chastised beyond compare.

Up the next bit of hill towards the forge and the sight of the flying red sparks from the impact of the hammer on the red-hot iron, almost though not as spectacular as the stars. Inside a farmer or two waited, the blacksmith kept hammering away, and burps from either front or tail gave evidence of the horse's agitation and nervousness. Soon you would be at home doing your lessons.

But the road got lonelier, less houses, then no houses at all, and the mental onrush of the imminent dangers – tinkers, kidnappers, the man-woman, the freak, or the man who dropped his trousers and said, 'Come here till I do pooley in you', and did it beside the pump, so that if anyone came he would pretend that he had decided to take a bath. Out of breath, satchel held onto as if a person, the last bit of road with not a cottage, not a tree, and the high wall bordering our land where someone had chalked

'Up the Farmers', and the big wasp-filled hollow tree stump, and the remains of the tree that had fallen long before in a storm. Then the stubborn gate with its screechy hasp, and its faulty hinge, fixed to the stone pier that had on its surface one tiny spot of smooth slate which required to be touched over and over again for good luck, but couldn't be, because of the urgent need to get home, but had to be because of the attendant bad luck, and so a ridiculous series of running back and forth to touch it, not touch it, re-touch it, running on, and then of course the biggest bogey of all, a brush with the supernatural, because under such and such a tree a man appeared, an old gatekeeper who had died of a wrong; then the cattle, their stares, their huge heads, their bulling and their bawling, the chips on their horns glinting in the sunshine, cattle bulling and bawling – and home to what? Once it was the tillage inspector who had come, and had to be appeased with tea and scones before being brought out to inspect the barely adequate patches of wheat and barley. Once it was a dead litter of mice found in the sack of 'black market' white flour, little mice all dusted over and clung together as they had been smothered. Or it might be windows spick and span, beautifully snowy lace curtains, a smell of wax and such a feeling of airiness and perfume as if even the artificial flowers had become imbued with a little life of their own. Sometimes it was one's hair being examined for nits: head bent over the kitchen table and the fine ivory comb scraping through, delving into one's scalp, and woeful exclamations as the lice dropped onto the newspaper and crawled about for dear life. They would meet their end by the press of a thumb nail. Too many lice and you would be carted off to the Shannon overnight. You believed that, being of a disposition to give as much credence to the impossible as to the possible.

Wonder was never far away. Wonder about Amy Johnson and whom she loved, or who groomed Mrs Simpson's hair, or the air raid shelters in London where people were said to do untoward things and strangers made free with one another. There were gruesome murders that were not connected with war at all, by a man who lured women into a bath. Pagan London. Pagan England.

One day there arrived a swarm of honey bees. They congregated in a wall in the kitchen garden, and plans were being discussed to catch them and put them in an old bee hive, and from then it was only a question of summer days for there to be honey for tea, combs of it all about the place, honey to be spooned up to one's heart's content. My mother and the workman went up, togged out in wellingtons, long trench coats, hard hats, gloves and muffler scarves, to ensure that no part of them would be exposed and prey to a sting. They looked like young people following the Wren bird so bizarre was their attire and even they themselves laughed at their gear, although there was no mirror downstairs in which they could survey themselves. There was only the shaving mirror positioned between two windows, the scene of many a tirade on Sunday mornings when my father got into a tantrum before going to Mass. They were to catch the bees in big roasting pans. My mother also brought a lovely black gauze fan that she was to usher them in with, if needs be. We could hear the kitchen garden gate close and then suddenly there was an earthrending scream followed by a silence and my mother's piercing question 'Oh Jesus, does he have two stings?' We heard later that the bee had got under her hard hat, and in her description of pain at which she was wizard, she said it was like nothing so much as a six-inch rusty nail boring through her. The enterprise was dropped and instead of spoons of honey it was back to the homemade jam, the bramble jam, and the slightly amber crab apple jelly, flavoured with spices.

The weather was better then or else time is stretched in fine weather and summer evenings and red-gold skies seemed to go on till midnight, and all the doors were left wide open, to let the breezes in. There were folding card chairs that could be carried around to the front of the house, in order to sunbathe. Once a young priest called unexpectedly, and I had to pull on my cardigan hurriedly and button it up. My mother laid a tray for tea, and kept imploring of him to please have two boiled eggs because look, she had a colander full of them. At first he demurred, said he had already had his tea, and must watch the avoirdupois. He put his pale hand across a chest that was clad with a beautiful black pleated shirt and where not a scrap of waste flesh lodged. So it was two eggs, a white and a brown, cooked to a T, and a special little egg spoon with a leaf motif on its handle, and salt from the cut-glass cellar, and freshly made mustard in the cruet, because along with the eggs she had brought a sensation, but *only* a sensation, of cold bacon, left over since dinner time. How we fussed over him, wheeling the tea trolley to the edge of the step, getting a second cushion for his back, asking if he liked milk first, calling him 'Father, Father' and later plying him with fruit cake, marble cake, and a slice of cold lemon meringue pie.

If there is such a thing as the birth of maternal instinct I discovered it that day wanting to do everything for him, even dreaming of washing his feet. I thought of Mary, Mary Magdalen and her ointment, I thought of her long dim hair. He was soon to go with the foreign missions, and in the silence that followed this grave declaration all the brightness seemed to go out of the evening, the light that a moment before had been dancing on the cut stone, and making each buff grain into gold as bright as the edging of his missal, was gone, vanished. We would never see him again, and would not know, would never know what lay in store for him, in that other continent with its dark interior and vile eating habits. He gave us his blessing before he left. We knelt on the stone, side by side, closed our eyes and awaited his blessed hands.

Once he was gone my mother was overactive, said work had been lagging, and she hurried to feed hens, to scald buckets for milking, to take the day-old chicks from around the lamp that was their replacement mother and sit on the edge of the big orange box watching while they pecked at the little bits of moist Indian meal. She too had felt some odd pang.

4 The books we read

SUCH THINGS occurred in books. Though not many books were in circulation. Two or three or four dog-eared volumes were passed around, loaned page by page, endlessly devoured by the women and endlessly debated over. Did he love her? Was she jealous of his governess? Was there a curse on the estate? Was the broken mirror the significant factor? Stories of men in morning suits, elopements, cashmere mantles, ladies with hectic flushes leaving meals untouched, eau de cologne, faints, cambric handkerchiefs, proposals, jealousies, cruel fate; stories of thwarted love because a man was married and marriage was indissoluble, or because a man had been married and the shadow not to say the curse of his former wife loomed over the bride's happiness; or thwarted because one or other were of a different faith and that was a dirament impediment, and the biggest obstacle of all!

A Miss Annie M. P. Smithson told such stories, painful and

breathlessly sad – a nurse in love with a man of the wrong faith, upon learning the fact disappears, goes through the throes of separation, uncertainty and temptation but after a long, chaste, and exemplary life is reunited with him and, naturally, he is converted. Or a corpulent parvenu with a mortgage on a beautiful old mansion salvages it by marrying the rosebud Clementina against her wishes. But of course he is discomfitted through the agency of a ghost and she finds the man of her heart. Always the 'Via Dolorosa' until the excruciatingly happy ending, until the miracle of everlasting love occurred.

One looked in the bone-backed hand mirror either before, during, or after one of these heady bouts to ascertain if some change had been wrought in one. Was one beautiful? The stuff of a heroine? Was it wise to put a clothes peg on the nostrils as Amy or Meg did in *Little Women*? Should one change one's name to Lydia? Beauty was of paramount importance. It decided one's fate, one's future and without it no Mr Magnetic was going to give one a second look. A lady had simply to look perfect, remain speechless and she had her man.

When Mr Carlisle, the exemplary hero of *East Lynne* first saw his future (his errant) bride he

> . . . had not deemed himself an especial admirer of woman's beauty, but the extraordinary loveliness of the young girl before him almost took away his senses and his self-possession. It was not so much the perfect contour of the exquisite features that struck him, or the rich damask of the delicate cheek, or the luxuriant falling hair; no, it was the sweet expression of the soft dark eyes. Never in his life had he seen eyes so pleasing. He could not withhold his gaze from her, and he became conscious, as he grew more familiar with her face, that there was in its character a sad sorrowful look. Never does this unconsciously mournful expression exist, but it is a sure index of sorrow and of suffering; but Mr Carlisle understood it not. And who could connect sorrow with the anticipated future of Isabel Vey.

On and on, forgetting supper, rosary or whatever, to discover that they were rapturously happy until snake jealousy took possession of Isabel, until misunderstandings engulfed them, until she ran away, suffered a disfiguring accident in a railway train in France and after several years came back incognito to be children's nurse in her husband's household. Her husband has married the woman she was jealous of, her heart was broken, she ailed, revealed all on her deathbed and the handkerchiefs of this world were soaking wet.

Nothing could be further from reality. The topped egg had gone cold in its cup. There was scum on the cocoa, a voice was saying, 'Have you done your exercise' or 'Get that table cleared'. Outside it was growing dark. The cows were already milked, there was half a candle left which you were enjoined to spare. You quenched it and, in the dark, thought all the more wrenchingly of poor Isabel and all she had to bear. Life was so tame beside that. The fields, the bog where the lilies grew, the parish of a thousand souls, the old canon delivering long sermons interrupted by coughs and phlegm, the pails of milk, the conversations were as dishwater compared with the nectar in these star-crossed tales. Miss Annie M. P. Smithson or Mrs Henry Moore, or some other enchanted creature was saying that the moon swam high in the heavens, that it dimmed indeed the stars, that they seemed to retire into thicker clusters, while such and such a couple stepped forward to enact the most vital, the most consequential drama of their lives.

The two worlds did not meet. Reality was a dull second. And sex the forbidden fruit was the glass coach in which to do a flit. Of course there were hardier stories involving war queens not beguiled by those first sweet hours but seeking the ultimate love and that after much battle. One did not identify as much with these ladies since they did not succumb. There were many names, high-sounding names like Deirdre and Emer and Maeve. But the one you liked was Macha the red-maned, stern-brown and minatory, no tender damsel this but red as if she had been bathed in blood, and with power over souls. With her lance she touched a sleeping king, and when he saw her he stood up on his feet and his whole soul went out to her and he proffered love and homage. Then in the forest when he sought to embrace her she bound his hands as a shepherd binds a lamb, having stripped a willow tree of its pliant saplings. She left him thus and did the same to the next and the next until the right one seized her in his mighty arms and she changed into a blooming maiden and responded to his love and became his bride.

One was already wearing the white veil.

Above the black range, a little framed prayer used to wobble back and forth in the draught from the chimney:

> *May the meals that I prepare*
> *Be seasoned from above*
> *With thy blessings and thy grace*
> *And most of all thy love.*

The meals were the mashed potatoes referred to as pandy, potato bread or boxty, and a concoction of potatoes, onion and cabbage called colcannon. To eat them was pure penance. To eat anything ordinary was. There were the blackberries glistening on the hedges but a glacé cherry was as precious as a jewel. There was a porter cake or the treacle cake that one turned up one's nose at, but a shop cake, a swiss roll say, stale as rice paper, spoke of another world where heroines stood at the casements in the sun's last beam, and were flushed with a deep suffusion of the crimsoned firmament.

People came, not quite fitting these majestic standards, but with different voices, toffs in plus fours, with sports cars, and once a lady with a big swansdown powder puff stitched into the centre of her spotted silk handkerchief. She brought little plasters for curing corns and they too had all the fascination of ornament. The central whorl of the corn came off in the little plaster and everyone marvelled. The men called her Betty, slapped her bottom and it was rumoured that she was not wife to any one of them, although she slept in their houseboat. They dapped all day, using the mayfly as bait, they ate picnic lunches, caught trout or failed to catch trout, carried their catch through the town in the evening to the hotel, where the scales were always ready so that the fish could be weighed. Then at night they sat in the hotel parlour drinking whiskey, asking locals to play the fiddle. Their vowels did not sound like vowels at all, but were squelched together. They called everyone Paddy and told dirty stories.

One week, parties of people clubbed together to go to Limerick to see *For Whom the Bell Tolls*. The film was a tear-jerker. The cinema was named 'Stella' after a guiding star, and had a huge carpeted restaurant where they served mulligatawny soup, sausages with peas, and iced cakes named after Toronto. The film's historic or political significance was cast aside, or never grasped, because what happened – so one was told – was that Ingrid Bergman loved Gary Cooper and had a baby in her while he was most treacherously shot. Ernest Hemingway's story was about Ingrid Bergman, and the guerilla Gary Cooper, staggering along a dyke with a bullet in him, telling her to live on. People described the story, but in no two instances were the details alike.

Yet up in Dublin a couple of hundred young men had gone off in blue shirts under the aegis of General O'Duffy to fight for Franco in Spain, but that was in no way related to Ernest Hemingway's lacrymose story. The village was sharply divided into those who voted for Cosgrave's party and those who were for Dev's. De Valera was the venerable hero. 'Up Dev', one read. It fitted nicely on the stone walls, or the back of the ball alley, or even the road itself prior to his occasional visits. Dev was a holy man, went to Mass and the sacraments every day, and spent a holy hour besides in a chapel in Leeson Street, no doubt examining his conscience. When Dev came and stood on the big lorry he wore a black overcoat as long as a priest's. He was austere, not like Paddy Hogan, the ex-minister for agriculture, who was a wit and a raconteur. Paddy Hogan had hecklers, a man said right up to him, 'How many toes has a pig, Mr Minister?', and Paddy Hogan said, 'Take off your boots and count them.' There was applause from everyone, even the people who wouldn't be giving Paddy Hogan their number one. The economic war had occurred long before, when beasts were let die in the fields, and an almost similar catastrophe when the foot and mouth disease took root, and some believed that the germs were sprayed into haysheds at night by British agents.

There was the Englishman who bought a big house down by the water, a lovely pointed cut-stone house with ornamental trees, red squirrels, owls, gongs and an indoor pump. He had it razed to the ground, sold the stone, and the marble mantelpieces, to the county council at a loss! Nettles grew out of the broken piers and the rooks were masters in the old trees that he had forgotten to fell.

There was the missionary who came and spoke in much more ecstatic, and at the same time much more incriminating tones, about the immortal soul, and on those evenings the picture of hell, the great chambers of hell with its tongues of blooded flame and its gleeful devils, stood out more clearly in some lonesome, damp, sweating, overcrowded chapel, than if Hieronymus Bosch himself had come in with his easel, and painted the infernal scene and picked people out, oneself, or one's parents, or one's friends, and pitched them into the bowel of that hell.

There were the fourteen stations of the cross depicting the route to Calvary, occupying both main walls, pictures as vivid as the bowls of pigs' blood that they made the puddings from. The women stuffed the blood into little colourless pouches, tied them at both ends and then simmered them slowly for hours, and served them for breakfast, the next Sunday, or next holy day, or the next special occasion.

Special occasions were the pearls of existence. Unexpected visitors – people even your mother was hazy about. Usually they came from the States and they would bring beads or baubles and boast about their houses.

They would be shown the bedrooms and then the outhouses, hayshed, cowhouses or mangers, and the chicken run; then back for tea and scones and brown bread and queen cakes and sponge cake and marble cake and fruit cake that in the cookbook was called plum cake. They would talk about crops, shortage of artificial manure and, to puncture the silences, my father would break into a song about the 'Maid of the Sweet Bron Ewe'. Then as a result of his revived spirits my mother would ask him to tell the one about the 'made' match and my father would prevaricate,

A school child

O hear me, Christ
Without stain, never
Let me be severed
  O Christ, from your sweetness!

Kilmainham Jail

Kilmainham Jail, 'the Bastille of Europe'.
The guard extending a very happy welcome
and saying that to appreciate it we ought not
to see it as a pile of stones, but a symbol and
a memorial of cruelty perpetrated on our little
country by an alien foe. Visitors included
some of the alien foe, Americans, and locals
who were distinguishable at once because
they cleaved together like figures of clay. The
rooms cold, cobbled and mortarish, bore the
names of their most illustrious inmates. It
was hard to conceive of Parnell writing as he
did to Kitty O'Shea, saying he was very well
treated, got a lot of sunshine in the morning
and was improving his skill at handball.

Boys mitching

Those boys might still be the protagonists of
James Joyce's story 'An Encounter': boys
who met after school to mimic the pitched
battles of the Wild West. Once a pair of them
mitch from school and escape into the country
where they meet a tramp, 'a queer old josser',
who describes to them fulsomely how he
would whip boys who had a sweetheart,
deliver a whipping such as never was seen
in the world before.

Kerry Men

Kerry men say they are the toughest men in
Ireland and masters at serving women, but so
do Cork men, Clare men, Roscommon men,
Mayo men and all Irish men – those whom
God made mad, for all their wars are merry
and all their songs are sad.

The man that had music in him
And in Kilkenny it is reported
On marble tombs as black as ink
With gold and silver I did support her
And I'll play no more till I have a drink.

Intoxication
'Ladies and Gentlemen, wheder dis hot or cowld,
'tis all de same, one drinks to be cowld, and anoder
drinks to be hot, an' 'tis mighty cowld it is in de end.
I first drank my own clothes in de pawn, den I
drank my wife's cloak off ov her back, den I drank
her flannel petticoat, den I drank de cups and de
saucers out ov de cupboard, den I drank de plates
and dishes off ov de dresser, den I drank de pot an'
de kittle off de fire, den I drank de bed-clothes from
de bed, and de bed from under meself an' me wife,
until dere wasn't a mortal haport dat wasn't turned
into gallons ov porter, an' glasses ov whisky, and
dandies ov punch! What brought me to my sinses
at last was the cowld flure, and de poor children
cryin', "Daddy, daddy, we're hungry".'
(Man taking the pledge.)

Such a man was always being written about by Myles Na Gopaleen: watery-eyed, scrampling out of his digs, making it to the Public, gripping a table to arrest the delirium tremens, calling for a ball of malt and water, spilling the water, swallowing the drink whilst his false teeth was clattering against the tumbler, and shrinking into himself when lo! some pedant fixes upon him and begins a peroration about the vices of cigarettes.

would finally tell how he brought Teddy the Protestant with the twitch to the next county to 'vet' three girls for his future bride. And how, soon as they got there, they were confronted by three girls in their finery, with puffed sleeves, necklaces and so forth. Then he would pause to see how engrossed the visitors were, as indeed they were. He would tell how Teddy chose one of them, how they were sent out to walk the grounds, to get acquainted, how meanwhile a buffet was announced, and the dining-room table yielded cold meats, pickles, beets, potato salads and all sorts of confections. The lovers were recalled and Teddy – having just downed a sherry – took a look at one of the other daughters, and said hesitantly, 'I've changed my mind, I think I'd rather have her.' Then everyone laughed. My mother said my father was a scream, and one of the visitors would ask who Teddy had married and the answer would be 'no one'. My father might conclude by saying that Teddy was a 'nice craytur'. Teddy had died, in his house, was not found for days. There would be some commiseration about that, and all the other untimely deaths, and it would be time for the next cup of tea, time to hold the cubes of snow-white sugar between the little tongs and to note how beautiful it was.

After the refreshments the men would go out to look at the animals and discuss what these might fetch at the next fair. There was a pig fair once a month, a cattle fair the day following, and on the main streets young pigs were kept in creels where they squealed non-stop, while the cattle were running and slipping and slithering all over the place. The farmers drank big pints and spat into their hands as they effected bargains, sometimes wiping the foam off their moustaches with the sleeve of their frieze coats. At dusk they would round up the cattle that were not sold and bring them back again to their holdings and their disgruntled wives.

The fairs were uncouth and for days the aftermath of the smell of dung hovered in the town and in the shops. The next excitement might be the arrival of a drama company and this would be announced on posters gummed to the shop windows, or on stone walls held down with a loose stone or two. There we would learn whether it was going to be Mr Anew

MacMaster bringing Shakespeare or the strolling players bringing soppier things. Mr MacMaster excelled in monologues and to see him flaunt about in his toga was to imagine being in Rome during the time of Caesar and Mark Antony. How he fulminated. No hoi polloi ladies were keen to sit in the front row, though they normally coveted those chairs because in his proliferations Mr MacMaster would lather their faces and their lapels with spittle and they would come out exclaiming how they were drenched.

Shakespeare was lofty, too lofty, but the melodramas were what touched the audience and wrung tears and shudders alternately from them. Count Dracula would have the entire hall of men, women and children gasping for breath. They would jostle with one another to see how Dracula inserted the safety pins into the girl's throat and got the veins open to suck the clean blood. Often in the aftermath people were afraid to go home and would have to be conveyed, but already they were worrying about the money for the next evening's performance.

Before the show proper the leading actors would be at the door, giving tickets, but eminently unreachable because of their reserve, their makeup, their crusted eyelashes, their sequined boleros, their frilled shirts and, above all, their beautiful throaty voices. All aspects of them seemed shown to perfection in the pathetic glare of the two paraffin lamps that served as footlights. Curtains might catch fire but who cared! It was 'All for Hecuba and Hecuba for me', as one actor was reported to have said one morning upon being given an egg with a foetus in it, for breakfast! In the town hall men, women and children cried, wept, snivelled, swallowed their own tears when the last scene of *East Lynne* was being enacted as an hour previously they had cried when a boy, little Willie, had died on stage and left a crazed broken-hearted mother.

Tenderness was one thing when actors did it, but quite lacking when a man told his wife to belt up or a woman had all her teeth drawn out in the side room of the hotel, to which a travelling dentist came once a fortnight, and was known for his cruelty and his prowess with pincers. It was different on stage, when in *South of the Border* the cowboy saw his lost love take her vows as a nun, saw her sitting on her little dais in a pool of heavenly light. It was permissible to cry then and everyone did, including the actors themselves. They had reputations for keeping late hours, for quarrelling and the women – who must have been addled with minding their children and cooking in one-room lodgings – were never seen out at all, until they appeared as the heroines, transfigured.

I knocked at the door of one such couple and remember so clearly, too clearly, the interior – children crying, some sort of meal in progress, and the actor in his shirt sleeves, looking at me with the most amazed, most irritated countenance, saying 'Scram', and then 'How did you get here?' I had come up the back stairs and he was happy to tell me that there were no vacancies for actors, actresses, stand-ins, ticket-takers but would I be kind enough to ask the landlady downstairs to send up a jug of milk and a glass of porter so that they could have their bloody lunch. Yet that night he was the possessed Dracula, and the dark room and the wan woman with the metal curlers, and the squalling children made no indent at all.

A story of 'love and murder' is how *The Collegians* was described. To us it was the story of Eily O'Connor, the flower of Garryowen, plucked from her father's home by Hardress the smart Collegian. Each chapter had its own alluring heading. 'Of the pleasure gardens of Garryowen.' 'How Kyrle Daly rode up to woo . . .' 'How Eily O'Connor puzzled all the inhabitants of Garryowen . . .' 'How the friends parted . . .' 'How the temptation of Hardress proceeded', and on and on. The night Eily left home, already married in secret, she threw her blue cloak over her shoulder and walked into the air 'but not before sadness had settled on her heart like a black reef'. From then on it was a case of deception, slight, separation and eventual downfall. On their first night, sheltering in a friend's house because of a storm, Eily had to be passed off as the sister of a servant, had to disguise her features, and sit upstairs in a little room while her husband was downstairs supping and dissertating on the ethics of life, with his friend and rival Kyrle Daly. Eily sent a message entreating him to come up:

The lovely ingenue who was employed at that moment in arranging and drying her hair felt her heart beat somewhat quickly and strongly at the sound. She threw back from her temples the wavy masses of gold that hung around them, and ran to the door with lips apart and a flushed eager cheek. 'It is he,' she exclaimed to her own breast as she undid the bolt. It was not *he*. The weatherworn freckle face of the little hunchback was the first object that met her eyes.

The same hunchback whom Hardress had instructed to get rid of her, 'To put her on the sthrame' and let her be washed away. He had had his fill of her and ordained that she be found dead. But her ghost avenged itself on his spirit.

Thackeray said that every hibernian tale left him with a sort of woeful tender impression. He was referring in particular to *Castle Rackrent*, Maria Edgeworth's novel about an eighteenth-century castle on Longford and its profligate owners. The life as with many of the squires was careless of expense, full of debt, as each owner lived for the day. The days consisted of hunting, shooting, swearing, duelling and incessant drinking. The first owner, Sir Patrick, died in a drinking fit; then Sir Murtagh burst a blood vessel while having an argument with his wife over money; Sir Kitt, more impecunious, was compelled to marry a crippled Jewess in order to pay his gambling debts. But she was canny, and refused to hand over her dowry which was contained in the thousands of diamonds which she wore about her person. As a punishment he had her locked in one of the large damp rooms where she had to while the time looking at her diamonds and eating the pork that for spite he had sent her to eat. After seven years her rescue came when her husband, after a duel involving his paramour, was trundled home in a wheelbarrow. Then came Sir Condy equally feckless and committed to the bounteous life. He acquired new horses and chariots, installed a theatre in the barracks, had his wife gorgeously jewelled and gave fine balls until at last he was deposed to the gate-lodge. He died having drunk a horn of whiskey to win a bet that would give guineas to his opponent and a mere sixpence to himself. He died delirious.

At any rate drink was the national sport and men were always stumbling through doorways or relieving themselves against a wall or inside the pub singing and calling for more. At Mass when the priest drank the wine in the white gold chalice the lads used to be holding their swallow and wishing Mass was over so that they could repair to the public. A medical student came home blotto, fell three times on the stairs, pretended he was really enacting Calvary and when he saw his suppliant mother, called out 'Jesus meets his afflicted mother'. The men laughed at that but the women said 'my﹍my'. Women did not drink or if they did it was port at a wake, well diluted with cordial both to look and to taste harmless. A man came home from the pub one Sunday, asked for his dinner and when his wife told him where to get it he took the carving knife to her and cut her from elbow to wrist. Under the influence men could do anything and even some members of the Garda had lapsed, according to the Superintendent who paid one of his annual though unannounced calls:

Visited station in connection with divisional tour. Sergeant M. Lennon 231 and station party present. When I arrived at the station the sergeant sat glaring at me and refused to call the party to attention. I called the party to attention myself and Garda O'Neill tried to rise but fell into the fireplace. I asked the sergeant to account for the state of affairs existing at the station and he replied in a manner that would do justice to the worst corner boy in the slums of London. I searched the barracks and found that a seizure of poteen had been made the previous day and had been consumed by the station party. The barrack servant sat with a baton, protecting the remainder of it and refused to move. She also had possession of station books and refused to hand them over or allow me to read or examine the books. In my examination of the station I found that the WC was filled with station records, apparently used by the station party on their visits there. I heard a noise coming from the cell and I went to investigate. I found three young ladies there from whom I took statements. They complained that when passing the barracks they were forcibly taken in by Sergeant Lennon and Garda O'Toole and Burke for purposes better imagined than described. In the kitchen of the station I found Garda Burke. He caught me by the uniform and refused to let me go till I promised to refund a fine of five pounds imposed on him and have records of same erased. When I returned to the front of the barracks I found the sergeant urinating into the front of the street from the front door. He started to argue with me on the footpath, with his private part exposed, each syllable was punctuated by bursts of urine against the road. On leaving the station I was approached by a local trader who demanded me to make the station party pay some of their debts for the preceding twelve months now amounting to seventy pounds. The whole situation at Corofin was disgraceful. I returned to Tuam and had the whole station party suspended immediately. I hope the divisional officer will ensure that these men discharge their local debts before they themselves are discharged from the force.

5 A convent

NO SUCH BARBARITY pervaded the sanctity of the convent environs. It was forty miles away and situated at the foot of a lake into which, legend said, a former hedonist city had been plunged and swallowed up. The town was grey and somewhat seedy and time seemed to pass slowly and without event. To go through the gateway and then hear the hasp being shut by the stooped gatekeeper was to take a step from which one could not retreat for five long years. The parents lingered in the reception hall talking to a nun and certain mechanical courtesies were exchanged. Then you were handed over, and the snivelling was dismissed by the nun with brusque and off-putting optimism.

Big spaces from now on – recreation hall, classrooms and refectory, rules for everything and nametapes on all one's belongings. The only escape came at dawn three mornings a week when we went to attend Mass in the Augustinian church and there one sometimes caught sight of the 'lovely priest', lost to us in his beautiful vestments and his mysterious Latin. Otherwise it was a world of women – nuns, lay nuns and little postulants and one was always seeing veils and starched headgear that framed the face and out of which eyes and nose peered as if out of a burrow. To see a nun's eyebrow was as wicked and as bewitching as Keats felt when he saw the ungloved hand of the woman he loved as she walked over Vauxhall Bridge.

Sins got committed by the hour, sins of thought, word, deed and omission, the sin of eating, nay devouring an illicit jam tart snatched from the cookery kitchen, the sin of smiling at a nun and having bad 'thoughts' about her such as brushing against her hand, the sin of sprinkling caster sugar onto the palm of one's hand and licking it to one's heart's content, the dreaded sin of consulting the mirror and then hawing on it to give oneself a dreamier look.

Once a year we were allowed out to the local show but there was about it a sort of unexpressed lethargy and disappointment, what with the muddied field, the winds (it was always October when the winds were said to lament), the men in their great coats, the women in their felt hats, the fillies and mares whinnying and rearing, the precarious showjumps and the spartan amusements (it was wartime) so that nothing quite lived up to anyone's expectations.

One of the vexations of later life is how carelessly we treat our elders. There is no regaining that time. There was the couple who had had a made match, who still kept the top tier of the wedding cake for the offspring that was not forthcoming. The wife was a distance away under an umbrella with a group of ladies, murmuring. He winked at me and said I was growing into a fine woman, then winked with the other eye, then nothing more. Standing there sucking the fibres of her scarf was a 'peculiar' lady who at times would burst into laughter and at other times accused people of laddering her viyella stockings with their diamond engagement rings. Except that there was not a diamond ring in sight, only the brown felt hats, the flecked tweed costumes, and brooches with lifelike similarity to beetles or spiders, brooches that were in vogue that year. The peculiar lady was just back from Lourdes and complained how everyone had to bathe in the same water, how it was not hygienic. Then she buried her face like a little girl in her fur collar, basked in it. I saw her twenty years later in a mental hospital, whereupon she asked me for a 'ciggy' and was playful as she had not been that day on the hill, when a horse bolted and the women became as hysterical as the children they were trying to protect. The odd toff had binoculars or a walking stick and one man with a black beard distinguished himself by wearing a faded green cape.

For refreshments we had lemonade, apples, and coffee-flavoured biscuits with a coffee icing. These biscuits required the accompaniment of hot tea to melt the icing slightly in the mouth so that the two extractions of coffee could be properly sampled and united. The apples smelt of nothing in particular out of doors, but back in the convent and just prior to Hallowe'en the parcels would pour in, be kept in the nun's little parlour, and to walk by there was to see them dimly through the frosted glass of the door and at once to imagine oneself in the ripest of orchards. Every girl's parcel contained a barmbrack and apples regardless of other treats and for a few days the convent acquired another smell and hence another atmosphere, whereby prayer and discipline and wax polish took mere second place and gorging was lauded.

Once after a nosebleed, when I had been laid on the red tiled floor and had keys and bunches of keys put all over my person, I was subsequently brought into that little parlour and told that I was a good girl, and given as reward a glass of lukewarm milk, which I hated. When the nun hurried out of the room to stop someone playing the piano in the recreation hall, I repaired to the vicinity of the three potted plants – a castor oil, a maiden hair and a bizzie lizzie, and doused each of them with the lukewarm stuff. I was still toying with the contents in the end of the glass when out of the corner of my eye I saw the milky liquid seep through the bottom of the terra cotta pots to the little saucers provided. Would she notice it?

'Have you thought of what you are going to be?' she asked with a certain coyness. Almost flirtatious was she. Oh to please her and win one's way into her hard heart and be invited to do little favours for her, like carrying her books, or opening or closing a window or cleaning the blackboards, oh oh to be her slave!

'A nun,' I said, quicker and more soulfully than I had ever said aught. The thought of a vocation danced before me; like a banner, the word waved and with it the vision of a young postulant with a see-through veil, one foot in the world and the other sinking deeper and deeper into the mists of spirituality, towards the 'never to be forgotten day' when one would take final vows and be cut off from the world outside, from family, from pleasure, from men, from earthly love, from buses and shops and cafeterias, from life.

'A nun,' she said, swollen with pride. Meanwhile I was brimming with tears that were as thick as glycerine, though not so nourishing.

From then on there was a subtle understanding I would become a nun and thus devolved on me extra duties such as to walk softly, to talk softly, to stay in the chapel after the others – the motley – had trooped out, to deny myself jam on Sunday, to drag my hair back severely from the forehead and therefore give no reign to quiffs or prettiness, to drink the senna tea without making a face, to read no delectable love story in the magazine that some day-girls brought in, to write a letter home only when one was permitted and to keep one's mind on such things as the visions of St Margaret Mary and the mortifications of the saints.

Parents seemed to exist no longer, or rather they had receded into being people who had given birth to one and about whom one had certain fossilised feelings, just as one day these nuns – the next instalment of parents – would recede and be replaced by another authority and yet another.

On Saturday night the head nun would read out to us something of moral, religious or political import. We would hear how St Bridget of Opaco achieved her destiny by going to join her dying brother in Tuscany, but not going as an ordinary traveller, rather in the middle of eating a meal of herbs and small fishes was transported across the sea by an angel. There and then she was told that she would have to set aside all earthly life and retire to a cave to live in austerity and penance. Or we would be told how bombs fell near Jaffa, that ancient city of the Bible, and how those bombs shattered the windows of a Franciscan monastery near which 'St Peter once so wondrously sojourned in the house of Simon the Tanner'. The next item might be that when the fishermen in Newfoundland felt their sight going they cooked and ate a cod's liver, or that poor Poland, the sister of dear Ireland, was in tears, suffering for faith and fatherland. And all over Europe that there was a bacon shortage. Then we were warned about literature, told how new writers were arch hands at depicting immodesty, in flaming imagery, relating the most obscene details, describing the worst carnal vices with subtle analysis and adorning them with all the brilliance and allurements of style so that nothing was left inviolate. Now that I was her favourite, I would carry her books and the weekly newspaper back to her desk, to the little parlour and there clandestinely I read a shocking letter discussing the favourability of studies from the nude, of sun baths, air baths and gymnastic exercises in which both sexes took part. The categoric answer was that the modern statuary of the nude or scarcely veiled statuary or photographs were all highly dangerous and that protracted gazing at such things without any just reason was usually a grievous sin indeed. If a painting had to be done on such a theme, then it was advised that all precautions should be taken, including the veiling of the sexual parts, the avoidance of mixed classes and the checking of ribaldry. Sun baths, and air baths taken by members of both sexes without costumes were fertile sources of sin it said, and gymnastics an offence against modesty.

I read it despite myself, then continued up the stairs to bed with legs sealed, hands clenched, armpits so close that not even a little flea could crawl in there. The same routine – shoes off outside the dormitory door, strategic undressing under the shelter of one's dressing gown and under the same awning washing in a basin of cold water, getting into one's nightgown and uttering further night prayers.

Most of the beds used to creak and some of the coarser girls would bounce up and down, the better to draw attention to this need for hilarity.

Sometimes slices of cake, a biscuit or a cherry might be covertly passed to one in the dark, and the pleasure of eating it was not a little mitigated by the realisation of the sin that was being committed, the sin that on some Cemetery Sunday in the distant future some soul would have to pray for in that communion of souls between living and dead.

There used to be the cups of hot senna on Saturday mornings and subsequently a great rush allied with a great anxiety for one of the four lavatories, that were situated on each of the four landings. Queues everywhere, girls holding their middles and swearing that they were not able to hold it, so that they could be let in next, fierce bangs on the door while they were having difficulty with the faulty chain. In her flounder one girl flushed a pink ten-shilling note away and when by coincidence the head nun said there was a great flush of money everyone burst out laughing, but no one could explain why in spite of her repeated and stringent enquiries. She sensed some foul unseemly plot and as a punishment we had to stand all next day for study, and those who coughed were singled out and put to stand near the rostrum facing the bulk of the pupils.

Jam on Sundays. I can still see it. A thin watery rhubarb jam, purplish in colour, sprawling along the side of the bread plate, getting in the way of the two slices of larded bread that had been hastily put down by the lay nun before she went off to do her other duties. Sunday was nice since there was the jam, a longer walk around the outskirts of the town, and in the evening we could get away with some little indiscretion such as wearing a white blouse or putting a slide in the hair. Girls fell in love with girls, squeezed hands or twined insteps under the long table while invariably remembering ahead to the little confessional, the mauve curtains, the sliding door and the priest's scrupulous cross-examination. Girls were in love with nuns and nuns either made pets or victims of one girl after another depending on their moods, and were prey to the fiercest kind of whimsy, probably due to their own troubles and the regulations to which they had to accede, regulations we knew nothing about. I used to look at my favourite nun and speculate on how much or how little a crop of hair was concealed beneath her guimpe and most improperly fell to thinking of what I had read about smoker's fur and how to ascertain if one had it. You had to run your tongue round your mouth and see if there was a rough woolly feeling there, in which case smoker's fur had got a hold on you and was staining your very teeth. If her hair grew again it would be like a little thatch of fur. My mind would make such speculation while she asked me how my vocation was coming along, or draw from her pocket a jam tart that she had saved for me. Often I felt we might kiss or that we might cry, but we didn't.

Not far away was the County Home, the abode of old people; men and women in different quarters, praying, sitting in the grounds, doing a bit of gardening or hoeing, sewing, trooping into their meals, some of them a bit soft in the head, latecomers getting scolded by nuns, looking forward to Friday, their pension day; they bought glacier mints and quids of tobacco. I with my vocation blazoned above my head was allowed to visit a nun there who was a distant cousin. She was small and enthusiastic and full of life. It was bliss being able to have tea in a little parlour, to drink it from maroon patterned china cups and to watch the serrated knife as she pushed it into the perfect sponge cake; wonderful to be party to her friendliness, to answer all her questions although she was already asking the next question, to eat to one's heart's content. Once she said that no, she would not have lived her life all over again had she foreseen its vicissitudes and I, full of strawberries and with the holidays looming, had no inkling of what she was saying, only that I adored her.

The day of the school play was magic with home rule for all. Classrooms were turned into dressing rooms, blackboards served as coat hangers with shawls and embroidered garments draped over them while dusters and chalk were slung in any old place. The smell that pervaded was excitement, perspiration and Pond's face powder. I was wearing a long toga and went on to recite 'Friends, Romans, countrymen, lend me your ears.' My favourite nun stood in the wings praying for me while I lamented Caesar's death and could hear backstage other girls laughing and cursing as they got into garments that they were unaccustomed to.

'The evil that men do lives after them,' I said, then paused to look at my enrapt audience. Never have I known such a hush and just then my nun said 'Brava' from the wings. Afterwards we exchanged presents, mine being a quarter-pound box of chocolates with two dancing kingfishers on the lid and hers to me a little illuminated card with serrated edges in which she predicted my future role as bride of Christ. Then she tickled my toes and we laughed and then it was time to be solemn because we were parting for the Christmas holiday.

The world outside and the rolling countryside seemed to emanate a beauty and the very hills seemed to breathe. All the deprivation had been worth it for this release, this return to the natural world. There was the holly with the berries just as in a happy Christmas story, there were the winter branches flushed with a promise of life, and Robin Redbreast going from hawthorn branch to blackthorn branch, to sapling to huge winter tree, chirping and not chirping; there were fields just glazed with frost and soon there would be the icing on a cake and the frail little mirrors of ice on a puddle, and five of us girls in a hackney car laughing and yelling at the sight of the driver's nicotined fingers. Somehow one knew that at Christmas one would smoke, go to one's first all-night dance, spin round and round in waltz or palais glide and go back to the convent with a secret to be shared with Lydia, the girl with the creamy neck and a long mane of hair which she sometimes held in a coil and slapped you with, as if it were a switch.

If going home was the greatest and the most incomparable of occasions, then going back a month later wreaked its full punishment because that day it was rain and wailing as one envisaged twelve more weeks of lard, cold corridors, accusations and severance from the hearth of life. Not ever able to step outside at night to look up at the stars, at the navy bosom of the heavens.

The next year or the one following I had the privilege of playing Our Lady of Fatima, my heavenly rostrum being six butter boxes covered with blue tulle. For a week curtains were thrown apart and I appeared as a vision while down below on the earthly stage, little children prayed up and asked for predictions about Portugal and the world. It was a part that called for utter stillness. Our Lady never stirred except that on the last night, due to the strain of standing, stage-fright, the wobble of the butter boxes which had not been properly fixed, an uncontrollable shaking took possession and like Humpty Dumpty I came tumbling down to the disedification of cast, nuns and visiting laiety. The performance didn't go on, and in the dormitory, biting my shame away, I hoped that no one would come up to sympathise with me, that no one would ever refer to it again and that I could simply vanish off the face of the earth. I wondered if it were not a punishment for some sin, the sin of pride, the sin of vanity, vanity resulting from admiring my pale pancaked face each night, and the body adorned in a beautiful blue and the importance of having been chosen to play the star role. I looked at one of the many pictures of the Virgin along the wall and realised that she no longer spoke to me as she used to when I was a child. The visions were waning.

The following summer an assistant who came to work in the creamery made a date and one night, resting against an iron gateway, I heard about A.J. Cronin while the love swain fumbled – first at the russet skirt, then the garters, then seamed stockings and then the blue long-legged satin knickers. I froze, whereupon he asked, 'Why wear such knickers, why doll up, why such provocation', and I could only say that I didn't know and the encounter was brought to an abrupt end.

'You're back early,' my mother said. I felt morose. She asked what in God's name had got into me since I was no longer the cheerful bubbling little girl. I demanded peaches. There was a huge can of cling peaches in a cupboard upstairs and only these sliding down my throat would satisfy my yearning. She asked if by any chance I had gone mad. I knew they could not be opened. They had been there for years, an heirloom, they were not for human consumption, they were ornaments to be proud of like the good cups or the good glasses or the plaster of paris ladies. Anger pervaded like a rash and there and then I knew that I would not be a nun, rather I would be a film star and get a perm in my hair and save up for an accordion pleated skirt, get high heels, perfume and fur-backed gloves. I distinctly heard W.B. Yeats call to me:

> *Come away, O human child!*
> *To the waters and the wild*
> *With a faery, hand in hand,*
> *For the world's more full of weeping*
> *than you can understand.*

But I turned a deaf ear.

Nuns at Seapoint, County Dublin

People say to one another 'do you think that nuns still wear
the long stockinette navy-blue knickers, or have they kept up with
the times and wear panties that match their new habits?'

The penitential beds at St Patrick's Purgatory, Lough Derg

Each week throughout the summer four or five hundred people wend their way barefooted around and about stone beds. Walking, kneeling, saying a particular requirement of prayers. To call them beds is to draw into question the numerous languid associations of that word. These are mediaeval cairns designed by some exacting sadist so that the stones, the points of flint and each chip of gravel perfectly pierces the soles of the feet where it seems most of our propensities are seated.

In the long ago princes, miscreants, sinners and travellers made the pilgrimage on foot from their own land, or continent, or homestead, and after a fast of fifteen days each one was locked in a cave for a night. During that lodging, many a one of these persons experienced ugly and ghastly visions as if in bedlam, 'with sprites clawing at him, tugging at him so ruggedly, tossing at him so crabbedly and now and then making him more frank of his bum than of his tongue', that often by morning he had passed out and the full office of the dead would be sung aloud until such time as he came back to earth, dimly aware of his ghostly voyaging.

Outside a betting office in Dublin

FIRST MAN: Did you put a few bob on the horse I told you – *Prairie Rose ?*
SECOND MAN: I did.
FIRST MAN: And? . . .
SECOND MAN: He stood up to shit and he's shitting still.

Spectators at Leopardstown Races

At the races were the 'law-di-daws' with cards and binoculars, the bookies with easels and blackboards, tick-tack men, and the bulks of people trooping around asking each other if they had had the winner. Mostly the men did the betting and the women and children converged in the stalls and booths where the vendors sold powdered lemonade, oranges, bone bangles, and where china dogs were put up for raffle.

Finbar Nolan, a faith healer — seventh son of a seventh son

There he was, a faith healer, a charmer, telling us that he must touch the flesh. A young boy whose looks are a combination of Georgie Best and the Giotto painting of St John the Baptist. He must touch the flesh. Off came jumpers, cardigans, stockings, frocks, corsets, brassieres, camisoles, vests, bodices and even scapulars. An array of white flesh, fat flesh, purple flesh, roly-poly flesh, every kind of flesh pitifully exposed in the weird torrential rain of a melancholy summer's afternoon in Ennis, County Clare. They talked to him in whispers, imparting more or less similar confidences.

'I have pains in my stomach and I have shingles.'

'I am stiff in my neck and I'm stiff in my shoulders. I'm stiff everywhere'.

'Down there now all along my legs, and at the butt of my back and could you put your hands on my veins could you, there, there . . .'

Holiday at Bundoran

Honky-tonky land of bars, boarding houses and amusement. A youth singing, 'Say that you love me'. In the ballroom assorted dancing, in the dining room a man with a drinker's nose requesting muslin through which to strain his port, and in a certain bar wanted IRA men awaiting developments. Further along the coast, under eerie magestic Ben Bulben the poet Willy Yeats turning in his grave because of the taverns, inns, and atrocious dishes that are being named after him.

Young love

A booklet called 'May I keep Company' says that people may plead about a chain of circumstances that has led to a brother and sister state of things, but that this may only be true when a certain age has been safely past or, if the parties like Our Lady had been conceived without original sin. But taking human nature at its average no fanciful relationships are much protection against real sensual passions.

A poor girl from Dublin's back streets

I'd wed you without herds, without money, or rich array.
And I'd wed you on a dewy morning at day dawn grey.

Said the great Sacrament here was dirt.

SEAN O'CASEY

6 Dublin's Fair City

THE LURE of the darksome wood and the hazelnut grove were giving way to a craving for glitter. The supreme joy of a secret game had gone – that game of repairing to the vacant room in order to teach shoes Irish and English recitations. It was no longer a thrill. Nor was that other hobby of collecting coupons of film stars and having ambivalent conversations with them. One could not stay forever, by the fire with its pictures and its sighs, or the people with theirs, or witness the eerie intimacy of a man and a woman at odds with one another, growling, yet sometimes paired in another room for two or two and a half minutes letting out sounds that very nearly bordered on despair. To go away. To run away if needs be. To put a big blanket over all those things, sighs and sounds, to forget voices and roars, to leave a note saying, 'I have gone with the razzle-dazzle gypsies, oh'. To pack a small attaché case and carry it down the drive, index finger over the lid lest the catches snap, saying a cruel, haughty goodbye to each landmark, treading for spite's sake on the harmless toadstools and puffballs, hitting the ash tree, the tree from whence came the series of plants that were used to belt animals and humans with. Goodbye to the humble little mounds, the ragwort, the chicken run, the dozy hens, goodbye to the tillage, goodbye to the green gate with its intractable hasp, goodbye to the ghosts wherein were contained all seeds of future laughter skittishness and woe. Goodbye to the ineradicable past.

Dublin was where I veered towards and eventually I got there, arriving by train, the suitcase reinforced with twine, the head full of fancy; conceiving of my destiny as being like that of a heroine who, upon being brought from Munster, faded in the city 'for consumption has no pity for blue eyes and golden hair'.

Dublin's fair city. I knew nothing of A.E., and George Moore, thought Yeats lived happily in a place called Innisfree (wherever that was), knew that blessed Matt Talbot, the builder's labourer, had collapsed and fallen to his death with a heavy chain around his body, knew that Sean O'Casey had written about people in tenements in the very streets where I cycled to chapel, to do the novena of perpetual adoration. Dublin had an abundance of bicycles at that time and when mine was stolen I despaired of ever finding it, and when weeks later I was summoned to a police station to identify it I found myself at a loss. All the bicycles being so alike with their worn, rain-soaked saddles, their battered mudguards and their little untwinkling tail-lights. Fortunately for me it had a number and was restored to me so that I carried on as before, precariously wending my way through O'Connell Street, to attend pharmaceutical lectures in Mount Street. There was a recitation current about bad driving and dangerous roads and I used to recite it to keep myself company:

> Some have died for love, some for the nation,
> But I'll meet my death through the Dublin Corporation.

Had I known that Yeats had described Maud Gonne's passage through those streets as being like that of a burning cloud I might have got off the bicycle in a spirit of worship, and emulation and said some little ditty to her. Working in a chemist's shop by day and attending lectures at night was a purely mundane and temporary pursuit. I could not decide whether to become a scholar or an adventuress, having little prerequisites to be either except a mane of hair, and a gentleman's white dress scarf bought at a pawnshop for tuppence.

The pawnshop was near Parnell's monument and one night walking home from a dance with an escort – a bread man from the firm of Johnson, Kennedy and O'Brien – we window-shopped and there in the pawn shop spread out like a peacock's tail was one of the two garments that I had possessed and that he had seen me wear – my bright, tartan, pleated skirt. We passed on to the butcher's further up and gazed at the joints of meat with the ruffed collars of fat around them and read the various arch suggestions for Sunday menus. Next we looked at the optician's and the magnifying glasses brought to mind old men leaning over tomes. Then there was a sweet shop full of bright round tins, tins with harlequins on the lids, and inside an assortment of sweets, all wooden but beautifully covered with silver paper and then twists of red glassette paper. We were almost always hungry and looking at these food shops we recounted situations in which we would be sitting down to dinner unfolding our napkins, smelling the gravy and in those teetotaller days pouring water from a big tumbler into slightly tinted glasses in which the water took on a hue of blue. At that time I had only tasted raspberry wine and its sweet cordial flavour was beginning to pall.

The bread man was a hurly player as indeed all the 'good catches' were. It was Croke Park for a hurling match, on Sunday, rain, hail or snow. We would always arrive hours early and already out of breath at the anticipation of the game, of watching various heroes slithering around scoring points or goals, even sometimes getting livid with each other on the pitch and resorting to fists. The pleasure was something not far removed from physical ecstasy.

The bread man had skedaddled but there were plenty of other dazzling men and it was hard to know who was the best looking, who was the king. We used to hover near their dressing rooms and hear the water splashing inside as they took their showers, and then lost our heads or our ardour as they came out, because never once did we push forward with the autograph book or the crushed violet that we had vowed to give. Instead and rather shufflingly we followed them down the various streets to the hotel where it was known that they imbibed and met their sweethearts and drank before going on to some dance or 'hop'. 'Come out now, missy, and I'll show you what life is all about,' a man said taking a grip of my arm and I had to run to the Ladies' for refuge and remain there in a tremor knowing he lay in wait. My best friend was inside jumping up and down with joy because she had just 'got her aunt' and was gazing into the lavatory bowl and vowing that we'd meet hurlers, that we'd meet captains of the team, that we'd strike up with horsey fellows, that we'd go places. Never was she so jubilant. She jumped with joy but what she saw in the lavatory bowl as evidence of her own menstruation must have been evidence of someone else's because three months later she had lost her job, and was living in digs with a devout woman who upbraided and re-judged her all the time and she was not allowed out, except for a short constitutional at night and in the company of her keeper. I used to visit her on Sundays without actually discussing what was happening to her. I could see that the one dress she had – a black one with appliquéd roses, was heaving out over her belly and she had coins ready for the landing phone and the number of a maternity hospital written on a little slip of paper which she consulted then folded and refolded until it was the size of a fingernail. But we talked about style. We were made for style. She said if only we could knit we would be fashion-plates. The intended 'father' was never mentioned, had no place save being the original furtive instigator in that tale of subterfuge and penance.

In the medical hall where I was serving apprenticeship my most flattering customers were the dummies from the nearby institution. They came and lounged about most of the day addressing me with sign language and sheepish looks, making plain their intention which was never to leave, but to be given barley sugars to suck and to squeeze my hand and imagine that they were in love. They were of all ages but the older ones stayed the longest and gesticulated the most with hands – a frenzy of hands, moving lips, spittle, excitement and beseeching eyes. I had two white coats, one with traditional lapels and the other with a high starched collar that buttoned at the throat and gave me the appearance of being a nurse in a romantic film. They were in no doubt about which one they preferred and used to clap when I wore it, especially on the day it came back from the laundry and was starched and crisp.

Some afternoons would just filter away and one would pass the time weighing Glauber salts into quarter-pound packets, or sifting worm powders into little envelopes, or writing price changes in the big sundries list. Life was at a standstill. Then again the shop would be full, children asking for tuppence worth of turpentine or gentian violet for thrush, men waiting for stomach prescriptions and whistling a little tetchily, babies being brought in for weighing and screaming beyond endurance when they were placed into the cold brass weighing scales. There would be people with little box cameras wanting their films changed, the phone ringing, housewives handing in their weekly order, oneself trying to do a hundred things and in the dreadful din the dummies would be sitting on their haunches smiling, glad that business had perked up because it would mean another barley sugar once the place had emptied.

Above the shop lived the owners and always for tea they had a plate of cakes sent in from the 'dainty dairy' nearby. Nothing was quite so enticing as seeing them laid out, some iced, some dusted with sugar, some with fruit or candied peel bursting through the crack, and the gallery tray laid for four. I often waited as the maid carried it down eager to see what was left and if I was lucky swiped a cake or at least crumbs that had fallen through the paper doily on to the plate. One day in the store room where I had gone to get a Winchester of something the boss came in to ask a question and as I tried to answer it, jam, mocha cream and crumbs fell out of my mouth.

The shame of that now brings to my mind the story of Chekhov being entertained in a grand restaurant in Moscow and suddenly spitting out a mouthful of blood. I had by chance found Chekhov and found the truest voice that I would ever know. Found the nourishment of reading and perhaps writing. I believe that memory and the welter of memory, packed into a single lonely and bereft moment, is the strongest ally a person can have. The further I went away from the past, the more clearly I returned inwardly picturing meadows, grasses, some animal caught under briars, cuckoo spit, nightfall and the way the dogs used to wear paint away off the back door begging with their bodies to be let in.

Night in the city was different, everything in the city was different. A dog was something that got walked in a park and its owner waited while it did the necessary, a dog was something that sat inside a window on its hind legs just looking out at the stream of life, whereas a real dog was something in a field barking, hunting, chasing rabbits, cousin to that noble beast who though held down by four men and as many chains broke through to kiss Ulysses, its long-absent master, and therefore prove his identity to those who thought he was feigning.

The city had numerous delights – clothes, cafés where ice cream was served in long-stemmed glasses and three distinct kinds of coffee.

'Two nice cups of coffee like the sweet American girls,' two GI soldiers were supposed to have said and the waitress was supposed to have asked if they wanted them black or white! A retort which everyone thought to be a scream and the very zenith of wit. Soldiers were to be avoided because after the rigours of war they were mad for girls. The few black men that strolled in or out of the cafés or the dance halls were to be avoided too, even though they were 'sheiks' in their own right. They proffered cigarettes which had dope in them. Medical students behaved wantonly, drank porter, cadged, skipped lectures and going home in the bus sang 'Gloria in Excelsis Deo' to the mortification of all.

My first foray into culture consisted of meeting a radio actor who tried to inculcate into me the mystery of nuance. He would say a sentence and I would be asked to guess the emotion he was trying to convey – whether it was grief or mockery or shock. 'My husband whom I loved very much has just left me' was the never to be forgotten sentence and by the intonation I was supposed to guess correctly whether it was as a grieved wife he spoke or an adulteress or a fading woman. But all the while – we were in a cafeteria upstairs – I knew that in the cinema down below they were showing *The Bells of St Mary's* and people were hearing Bing Crosby's voice, and beholding that face that I thought of as resembling a rueful fox. I knew exactly the moment when Bing hesitated and came back to say goodbye to the nursing nun and how my friend had hollered out 'Back for a guzzle, Bing!' and the irate people in the cinema said 'Shhhh' as her remark interfered with the gravity of the emotions. I longed to go down and sit in the stalls and see it all over again, the pure nurse, the hospital beds, the drifting snowflakes and the voice that somehow caught in one's throat. But I had no money. Money was the bogey, money meant everything – clothes, stockings, a hop, air-whirled powder, mascara and possibly nuptial bells.

The week's highlight consisted of going to a certain cinema where there was a stage show beforehand. Here was all the paraphernalia I longed for – slit skirts, suntanned thighs, boleros, sequins, saucy looks, legs askew and whole bevies of girls acrobating gracefully while covering their more pertinent parts with fans or gigantic powder puffs. It was always afternoon – my half day – and I went unaccompanied the better to take part in this secret feast. The lights would be silver or silver spun with gold, the orchestra sweet sounding, its conductor dressed in august black and on stage those creatures rouged, frail and full of the most unattainable mystery.

And as if that were not enough one soon learnt that these trifles, these human dolls were merely the backdrop to some 'cinch' who sauntered on, in off-white or creamy beige, and spoke directly and lovingly and heartfully to each lonely one of us as he sang, 'Brush those tears from your eyes and try and realise that from now on I'll always be yours.' The applause was so great that he sang it again. Nothing mattered. One could sit there, loll to one's heart's content, forget about hunger and study, one could cry, and then laugh at what the dwarfs did and then go backstage and watch them all file out and at last be thrilled at the sight of the crooner bending down to put on his bicycle clips. The fawn or cream suit would be exchanged for something more practical and after my fifth vigil there I was the happy receiver of a wink. Not long after an invitation materialised to his dressing room. I was laid carefully back on to the black horsehair chaise longue, a long kiss was delivered, followed by a deep feeling of misapprehension intermingled with delight as the fawn shoulders and the richly pancaked face bore down on me. The note on his mirror said 'I love you, Sue'. Who was Sue, was she Sue, Sue, Ciddy Sue? His thighs pressed deeper and deeper, the horsehair filling made its prickles known and as he adjusted himself perfectly to the proportions of my appalled body I felt everything melt except my troubled conscience. Then stiff as the proverbial poker I heard as though from Satan the most sickening of remarks, heard him say 'I could go through you like butter.' But my guardian angel was always presiding! There came at that very moment a knock on the dressing room door. It was the stage hand to say he had but five minutes before going on. Other girls were already out there in the dark awaiting the opportunity to swoon. When I asked if I could come back later he said, 'No chance, baby.' His wife was expected to arrive with sandwiches and a flask of tea. His wife was a peroxide blonde. I lay in wait to get a gawk at her. Perhaps she was Sue.

The next week he had a striped seersucker suit and sang 'I'd like to take you on a slow boat to China', while cradling an imaginary waif in his arms. Then another singer came, a Latin American, even more bewitching with gold fillings in his teeth and tattoos on his hands and his chest. He not only sang but he danced – peculiar dancing, using hands, inventing shadows, and doing loops into the air. That, you were told, was choreography.

Yes, you were going downhill. You had strayed far from the memory of the reality of the ellipse-shaped wounds of Christ, you found yourself living for these weekly delights where on screen you could witness 'the dallyings

Rugby players

Some former heroes limbering up at a pitch in Monkstown, near Dublin.

PREVIOUS PAGE

Brazen Head Hotel – Dublin's oldest pub

Behind the counter the proprietress supped tea. The place
was full of furniture, old chairs stacked on top of other old
chairs, a sideboard, bits of sacking, things. On the tiers of
glass shelving were the usual drink bottles, the usual empty
bottles, and a candelabra of artificial dust-thick flowers.
It was here that Robert Emmet plotted his revolution, it
was here that young Irelanders sat, it was here that a
highwayman scratched his name on the bottled-glass
window before he escaped. The famous clock and the
famous table are put away. A little push-bell says:
'Housemaid's bell only' and the corridors lead to locked
rooms where there are no longer, or where there seemed
to be no longer, any guests. This is Godot land.

Dublin Boot Boys

They are some of Dublin's
teddy boys standing in front of
St George's Protestant
Church that is modelled after
St Martin-in-the-Fields.
A few yards away is one of
Ireland's famed fortune tellers
and as you approach the block
of flats, children break away
from their games to escort
you to her.

The Liberties

The oldest inhabited quarter of Dublin City, served by the rivers Dodder and Poddle,
a seat of churches including St Patrick's Cathedral where Dean Swift is buried,
and where his epitaph is enough to dismay either tourist, pilgrim, or historian.

> *Here he lies*
> *Where fierce indignation can no longer rend his heart*
> *Go follow his example if you can*

A Pickaroon
Down the docks a young girl goes to forage for lumps
of coal. She is nearly always lucky because they overload
the lorries, and bits of coal drop off.

OVERLEAF

The Road

Forever you go towards silence further and further, it at once calls and repels. They will tell you Ireland is green, four green fields to symbolise the four provinces, but they will forget to add that in the winter months the fields are churned up because of the incessant rain and the hooves of the stampeding cattle, so that when the men do fodder, in the evening, after dark, they have to put the bales of hay upon the hedgerows just like bits of clothing, bales of hay for the cows to grab at.

Shadows of men among horses

A recitation was delivered with eighteenth-century gusto by a local farmer. A long poem about a man who had a pain in his teeth, went to the dentist, got a new tooth which fell out on the plate, came back for compensation and the two of them engage in a terrible argument until a pistol is produced and the patient goes home scratching his pole and sticking the old tooth back in the hole in his mouth.

The man who recited lives alone because his wife is in England with her nerves. He is douched in perfume that smells of incense, says he doesn't like 'th'oull sweat to smell'. The pattern of his life is that he farms, buys and sells a few cattle, that kind neighbours give him his Sunday lunch, that he fills up with a few pints every night, goes home drunk and gets under the covers with 'th'oull hot water bottle'.

There are certain things you cannot do for people . . . you simply cannot.

of divorcees and the lurid radiances of eroticism in bold Technicolor'. Not only that but you allowed yourself to re-live the swoon of the horsehair sofa and the complete unconsciousness of the body up to the dreadful moment and his prophecy of being able to go through you like butter. Intrigue was becoming second nature to you. Even while kneeling at your bedside to impress the other girls with whom you lodged, your mind wandered into those valleys of delight, already conjecturing about next week, his attire, the girls' thighs, the celluloid story and what might unfold.

In the paper you saw mention of the type of person you were becoming – 'the hot number with hair elaborately coiled and snowily peroxided, a slut with eyebrows gone and pencil lines replaced, a brazen strap with a mouth like the squeezed cross section of a bloody sausage.' As it pointed out you were one of the many who waited in cold wintry rain, in the queues, listening to the hanging signs swinging and creaking, willing to put your last shilling into the maw of the box office, in order to go in again and lose yet another ounce of your irreplaceable integrity. The theatre was unattainable since this required an escort. But it too had a sinful appeal. You read that the works of Eugene O'Neill were replete with 'murder, suicide, insanity and suggestion of sexual aberration', that Eugene O'Neill 'was a mess of pseudo-psychology with flub-dub dialogue'.

There was, but I was not party to it, literary talk, no doubt darned with invective in the Dublin pubs and lounges, and after closing time in the bona fides at the foot of the mountains where a rapid intoxication was mediated by the ingestion of crubeens or pigs' feet. Along with the drinking men, who were 'literati', was the opposite camp called 'bun men' and these with their acolytes repaired to the coffee houses but died just as suddenly and just as unaccountably as the topers. Serious-minded men on the Dublin Corporation were coming to the grave decision of rejecting Rouault's *Christ Crowned with Thorns* as being too obscene, and a man who had been to England on a visit brought back a set of false teeth that he swore had belonged to T. S. Eliot.

I went down the quays, to Finn's Hotel – where Nora Barnacle had been a chambermaid when James Joyce was courting her – looking vaguely for the dining room where my parents had celebrated their wedding breakfast. It was their anniversary. I did not cross the threshold, but stood, holding on to the bicycle, looking and waiting, certain that before the night was through something fateful would have happened. Perhaps we engineer these things. I went up along the quays, in a drizzle, past the nine chapels, blessing myself mentally, unable to remove my hands from the handlebars for fear of toppling over, past the shop that sold secondhand mantles and gowns and towards the bridge which was a hub of activity because the buses parked there and conductors and drivers changed shifts. There was a newspaper office not far away and I went down on impulse. I had entered a literary competition and was eager to know if I had won. Men stopped me on the stairs to say 'Laudamus te' and come to the tavern. One said that he hoped I was not called Sheila or Oona or Moura or anything Ballyhooly like that. I had pierced ears and wore gold-plated danglers at which he marvelled and said they would make suitable rings for a sow's nose. I had had the ears pierced one half day, sacrificing the time and the money from that beloved haunt, the cinema, and the doctor to whom I went had told me irately that when he pierced one if I let out as much as a miaow he would refuse to do the second. He too saw in me, or in my light-hearted action, the seed of something that would precipitate ruin.

In the pub I was the blushing toast of all the men and one was kind enough to ask if I wanted a packet of biscuits. Erudite men talking above my head about spondees, discussing the finer merits of malt whiskey, the Portuguese pox, the metaphysical madness of Kerry men as opposed to the apocalyptic madness of Clare men. They were bidding for me with drinks, gin and tonic, gin and white lemonade, gin and 'it'. The room was beginning to sway pleasantly and with the bob of the hanging lamps and the sight of the Liffey water I began to imagine I was on board ship and like the person in the song 'bound for Americay'. There were fog horns sounding too and as closing time was being bellowed out a decision was reached that we repair to an all-night shebeen run by ladies. A man with what I thought of as a Peter Abelard face was paying particular attention to me, telling me a long story about being at a remote railway station two-thirds drunk when a passenger leaned out of the window and asked him was he looking for the Flower of Garryowen, and together we talked of the Colleen Bawn, the lowlands around Limerick that are nearly always flooded and the plaintiveness of Gerald Griffiths' story that was set there. Then he sang 'The Captain with the Whiskers' and in the hush that followed after the applause a quiet man nearby, with an English accent, told me how he had been one of those responsible for getting Dev out of prison, he put the key into the cake with which Dev foxed the authorities. I was living at last.

I went back to the chemist shop full of grudge. The dummies got on my nerves, gentian violet stained my hands, and I mixed prescriptions in the old chipped mortar with something bordering on frenzy. He rang. More meetings in pubs and the erudite talk going blissfully, like a serial, and the changes, as they say, rung in my attire, by the borrowing of a red muff and then again a baby-blue crocheted scarf.

He was of the opinion that his friends lusted after me. I made one of those statements that are only made in the thick of juvenilia, and though true, must in the lull of life be ever after thought of as untrue, as trite. I said in answer to his suspicion, that if you have something for someone, you do not lightly give it over to someone else. He took my hand. That was all he needed to know.

But what had I? And what was I about to surrender. The meetings got more and more contorted and were in pubs at considerable distance from the city centre. Then one night he proposed we take a single decker bus out of town to see the hedgerows and the leafy lanes. Ripeness may be all, but at that moment in time surrendering oneself in a field had more to do with inexplicableness than the idea of ripeness or pleasure. Had one not been born, bred and raised to believe that this was the ultimate crime, constituting a smear of the body, a possible pregnancy and adieu to the friendship of God. Lost both in the corporal and in the spiritual world. Had he not been born with the same set of warped incantation except that men had more bravado than women.

I accompanied him to a restaurant where I refused food in case he could not afford it. I sat, watching him eat chips, sausages and peas, not with any gnaw for food but with a longing to ask what had happened. Was that it? Was the maidenhead, the precious gem, lost in such uncelebrated mire. Pirandello had said that somewhere a man was leading his life but he was ignorant of it. I felt the same watching my man's studious face and blond eyelashes, detecting his slightest trace of irritation as the peas refused to be stationary on the fork before he got them into the cavern of his mouth. We made a date for the following week but his interest had lagged.

A week later I stood at O'Connell Bridge leaning against a wall. There was an oil rig in and it was November. Fog horns, church bells and 'a desperado man' who amused himself by jumping off running buses and shouting 'bang bang' to the world. I paced back and forth, oblivious and yet not oblivious. A bus would pull in, people would stream out while I was pushed out of their way, and still no sign of him. The neon with a different gawdy light for each digit announced and re-announced the word BOVRIL. The sky had the usual sullen flush of a city sky at night. I waited knowing that he was not coming, and yet unable to budge, not out of hope but the better or the most excruciatingly to live out the pain of the first conscious jilt.

It was to be years before I read Kierkegaard and got a glimpse of the possibility of the triumph that can attend rejection, with the sure knowledge – that has nothing whatsoever to do with revenge – that those who feel and go along with the journey of their feelings are richer than the seducers who hit and run. The first mawkish poem came to me there and then, and repeating it aloud became for myself some sort of solace and an inducement to go on. It said:

> *Dark is kindly*
> *Making madonnas out of all their faces*

Giving ghosted bricky places
A peculiar pulse of life
And melting you
Until those brown eyes
Whisper lies
That the phenomenal heart
Afterward dies.

Not too long after I was whisked away by another, and like Lord Ullen's daughter, defied family and friends, did not drown, but rather repaired to a lonely bastion in the mountains overlooking scrub, heather and a freshwater lake. The sound that most often re-reaches me from there is the belling of the stag in the pinewoods at dusk. It had in it the very essence of youthfulness – sexuality, need, solitude and a threat. I had gone from the country to the city, then back to isolation again. For all eternity. The early mortifications, the visions, endless novenas, the later 'crushes' on hurly players, the melting glands at the cinema, the combined need for, and dread of, authority had all paved the way and it was in a spirit of expiation and submissiveness that I underwent that metamorphosis from child to bride.

7 Escape to England

LEAVING IRELAND was no wrench at all. I took the mail boat, like most others, sat up all night, watched the drinking, the spilling, walked the deck, remembered how Mr Thackeray and Mr Heinrich Böll had come in by boat to write leisurely about it, remembered the myriad others, natives, who had gone out to forget. Euston Station was a jungle, grim and impersonal, the very pigeons looked man-made, and when I saw the faces of the English I thought not of the long catalogue of blood-letting history, but of murder stories I had read in the Sunday papers and of that swarthy visiting English woman from long ago who brought corn caps and a powder puff stitched into her hanky.

This was to be home. It had nothing to recommend it. Unhealthy, unfriendly, mortarish and to my ignorant eye morbid because I kept seeing wreaths and did not know that there was such a thing in England as Remembrance Sunday.

But I had got away. That was my victory. The real quarrel with Ireland began to burgeon in me then; I had thought of how it had warped me, and those around me, and their parents before them, all stooped by a variety of fears – fear of church, fear of gombeenism, fear of phantoms, fear of ridicule, fear of hunger, fear of annihilation, and fear of their own deeply ingrained agression that can only strike a blow at each other, not having the innate authority to strike at those who are higher. Pity arose too, pity for a land so often denuded, pity for a people reluctant to admit that there is anything wrong. That is why we leave. Because we beg to differ. Because we dread the psychological choke. But leaving is only conditional. The person you are, is anathema to the person you would like to be.

BUT TIME CHANGES EVERYTHING including our attitude to a place. There is no such thing as a perpetual hatred no more than there are unambiguous states of earthly love. Hour after hour I can think of Ireland, I can imagine without going far wrong what is happening in any one of the little towns by day or by night, can see the tillage and the walled garden, see the spilt porter foam along the counters, I can hear argument and ballads, hear the elevation bell and the prayers for the dead. I can almost tell what any one of my friends might be doing at any hour so steadfast is the rhythm of life there. I open a book, a school book maybe, or a book of superstition, or a book of place names, and I have only to see the names of Ballyhooly or Raheen to be plunged into that world from which I have derived such a richness and an unquenchable grief. The tinkers at Rathkeale will be driving back to their settlement by now I say, and the woman who tells fortunes in her caravan will be sending her child down for the tenth loaf of sliced bread, while a mile or two away in her domain Lady so-and-so will tell the groomsman how yet again she got her horse into a lather, and on some door in a town a little black crêpe scarf dangling from a knocker will have on it a handwritten black-edged card stating at what time the remains will be removed, while the hideous bald bungalows will be mushrooming along the main roadsides. The men will be trying as always to distance their fate either through drink, or dirty stories, and the older women will be filled with the knowledge of how crushing their burdens are, while young girls will be gabbling, to invent diversion for themselves.

It is true that a country encapsulates our childhood and those lanes, byres, fields, flowers, insects, suns, moons and stars are forever re-occurring and tantalising me with a possibility of a golden key which would lead beyond birth to the roots of one's lineage. Irish? In truth I would not want to be anything else. It is a state of mind as well as an actual country. It is being at odds with other nationalities, having quite different philosophy about pleasure, about punishment, about life, and about death. At least it does not leave one pusillanimous.

Ireland for me is moments of its history, and its geography, a few people who embody its strange quality, the features of a face, a holler, a line from a Synge play, the whiff of night air, but Ireland insubstantial like the goddesses poets dream of, who lead them down into strange circles. I live out of Ireland because something in me warns me that I might stop if I lived there, that I might cease to feel what it has meant to have such a heritage, might grow placid when in fact I want yet again and for indefinable reasons to trace that same route, that trenchant childhood route, in the hope of finding some clue that will, or would, or could, make possible the leap that would restore one to one's original place and state of consciousness, to the radical innocence of the moment just before birth.